Arson About

Mark Wheeller

Nelson Thornes
a Wolters Kluwer business

Text © Mark Wheeller 2004

The right of Mark Wheeller to be identified as author of this work has been asserted by him in accordance with the Copyright, Designs and Patents Act 1988.

All rights reserved. No part of this publication may be reproduced or transmitted in any form or by any means, electronic or mechanical, including photocopy, recording or any information storage and retrieval system, without permission in writing from the publisher or under licence from the Copyright Licensing Agency Limited, of Saffron House, 6-10 Kirby Street, London EC1N 8TS.

All rights whatsoever in this play are strictly reserved and application for performance, either amateur or professional, should be made before rehearsal to MBA Literary Agents Limited, 62 Grafton Way, London W1T 5DW.

Any person who commits any unauthorised act in relation to this publication may be liable to criminal prosecution and civil claims for damages.

Published in 2004 by:
Nelson Thornes Ltd
Delta Place
27 Bath Road
CHELTENHAM
GL53 7TH
United Kingdom

08 / 10 9 8 7 6 5

A catalogue record for this book is available from the British Library

ISBN 978 0 7487 9010 4

Cover illustration by Paul McCaffrey, c/o Sylvie Poggio Artists Agency
Page make-up by Tech Set

Printed in Croatia by Zrinski

Acknowledgements
The playwright would like to express his appreciation to the following people: Tom Carr, Tim Murell, Donna Smith and Les Vivien from Hampshire Fire and Rescue Service. P.C. Darryl Saxton, Hants Constabulary. Martin O'Neill, Kent Police. Kemi Egan and Sophie Hall for wisdom on photo-love stories! 'Halloween Jack' (a lifelong inspiration) for a location – can you spot it? Saul Jeavons for the title. Evie Efthimiou and Saul Jeavons for their help and support in the initial drafts of *Arson About*. OYT 2003 ('Stars' group), particularly Danny Sturrock for assistance in developing the fairground scene. Andy Kempe for his suggestions which helped develop the play for this publication. Meg Davis and all at MBA for their continued support and belief. My wife, Rachel, and children (Ollie, Charlie and Daisy) for love and support ... and tolerance of long working hours.

CONTENTS

INTRODUCTION	4
FOREWORD	5
ARSON ABOUT	7
CAST LIST	8
ACTIVITIES	
Things to talk about	82
Things to write about	84
Bringing the play to life	89
Staging the play	91
Exploring the issues	94

INTRODUCTION

SuperScripts

SuperScripts is a series of plays for use in the English classroom and the Drama Studio. The plays have been written by professional writers who share a delight in live performance and the challenges it offers actors, designers, directors and, of course, audiences.

Most of the plays in the series were written for professional companies but all are included because they tell stories and use techniques which will interest, excite and offer new insights to young people who are just coming to understand how drama works as an art form.

The range of plays in the series addresses the requirement to give students at Key Stages 3 and 4 an opportunity to study a variety of dramatic genres. The fact that they were all written for performance (and have indeed all been performed) means that they will also offer students the chance to understand how and why playscripts are different from novels. The activities presented along with the script are designed to draw attention to this and to extend students' abilities in reading, writing and, of course, performing drama.

Many of the tasks invite students to use practical work to engage directly with the text or to formulate their own creative responses to its form and content. Others focus on the importance of discussing, writing and designing. Both English and Drama specialists will find the series a valuable resource upon which to draw in order to promote dramatic literacy. Of course, performing the plays wouldn't be a bad thing either!

FOREWORD

Every day three schools in the UK are damaged or destroyed by arson. The estimated cost of this in 2003 was over £100 million. Sometimes the cost is higher. Not so long ago three boys were trapped by a fire they had set and were killed. What can't be quantified is the hurt caused to pupils, teachers and the local community whose work is destroyed and who often feel that the arsonist has taken something out on them personally.

Mark Wheeller is already well known for his documentary style plays on subjects such as road safety, so it wasn't surprising that he was commissioned to tackle the issue of school arson attacks for a professional theatre-in-education tour. He writes that, *'unusually for me, the first thing to be decided was the title. In a preliminary meeting someone quipped that it should be called "Arson About". I seized on this idea, feeling relief at having stumbled across what I thought was a perfect title.'*

Many of Mark's plays use first hand accounts of events as the basis of the drama. In this case though Mark wanted to try something new.

From the outset I wanted to create Arson About *rather than develop another docuplay from any actual event. I had a number of brainstorming sessions with the fire-fighters in the Hampshire Fire and Rescue Service. By the time I returned home I had mapped out the idea of how the fire was set. The next stage was to spend time at the computer writing. In previous 'docuplays' my starting point would be interviewing the real people and getting their 'take' on whatever incident was to be retold. In this case I initially structured a story from Molly's point of view then retold the same story from the perspective of the other leading characters who each gave their own take on the invented events. A final idea was introduced by accident. I went to see the film* American Beauty. *This film was narrated by someone who had died. I thought this was an intriguing idea and one I wanted to incorporate into this play.*

As so often happens to projects such as this, the situation changed and the play, as it was then, was not performed after all. However, a good idea is always worth hanging on to so when, three years on, I met Mark

Foreword

to talk about what he might have in his filing cabinet that might make a good SuperScript, he quickly suggested *Arson About*. From my point of view the play touched on a nerve. It's not just because school arson is such an awful thing for so many pupils and teachers who like school (indeed, for many young people, school is one of the most secure and happy places they know; take that away and what have they got left?). It's also because it addresses the great paradox of youth. Young people want to find out 'What would happen if … ?' It's an attitude that teachers and parents should encourage. However, sometimes, in the quest for finding out 'What would happen if … ?' young people can get into deep trouble or, worse still, physically, emotionally and socially damaged. Ninety six per cent of police cautions for arson are given to youths aged between 10–19 years of age. There's a fine line between finding out and arsing about. Sometimes, young people don't see where that line is until it's too late.

The play presented here has developed a great deal from the original script. Why? Well, because Mark's ideas moved on and the audience, that's you, is different from the one he was originally writing for. An important strand of this development was to develop a dramatic narrative that kept the underlying message clear while offering a range of possibilities for performance and practical exploration by young people themselves. He writes, *'It has been a challenge and one I have enjoyed … but the proof of the pudding is in the eating. Will it work on stage? That is probably the most important phase … and I can't wait to see it! Good luck to all those who choose to work on it.'*

Mark Wheeller
Mark Wheeller teaches drama at Oaklands School in Southampton as well as running courses for teachers nationally. His plays *Too Much Punch for Judy* and *Hard to Swallow* have been performed by professional companies and schools around the world.

The series editor
Andy Kempe taught Drama and English in comprehensive schools. He is currently the Director of the PGCE Secondary Course at the University of Reading. His books include *The GCSE Drama Coursebook*, *The Script Sampler* and (with Lionel Warner) *Starting With Scripts*.

ARSON ABOUT

CAST LIST

Cashier	
Shuttle	13–14 year old boy, an individualistic (or freakish)
Narrator	
Molly Dukes	a 13–14 year old girl
Ian Thorpe	Molly's 13–14 year old boy-friend
Mr Butcher	Molly's and Ian's teacher
Chris Dukes	Molly's dad, a fire-fighter
Debbie Dukes	Molly's mum, a teacher
Nan	Shuttle's grandmother
Stuart Ricketts (Stueey)	a teenage tearaway, 13–14 years old
Stall Holders	just as you'd find at any fairground
Chorus	
DC Martin Ford	
Police	
Mortuary Attendant	
Ian's Dad	

Arson About was first performed by the Westgate School at The Theatre Royal Winchester on May 26–28, 2004. It was sponsored by the Hampshire Fire and Rescue Service as part of their drive for arson reduction.

The **Narrator's** lines could be presented in a number of ways: by an actor on stage, as a voice-over, as a PowerPoint® projection. The style should parody a teen photo-love story. The **Chorus** is commenting on the action which is sometimes in Molly's mind, sometimes outside but it is always involved as much as possible in presenting interesting physical images on the stage!

The play can be performed by a much smaller cast. This would involve the actors distributing the Chorus lines between themselves and perhaps cutting out minor characters such as Ian's dad and the mortuary attendant. The following doubling may be used as a guideline. Here, is a 2m 2f casting:

Male 1	Ian, Police
Male 2	Stueey, Shuttle, Mr Butcher, Chris, DC Martin Ford, Police
Female 1	Molly
Female 2	Cashier, Narrator, Debbie, Nan

1 Embers

*A **Cashier** stands at a till in a petrol station kiosk. **Shuttle**, an individualistic teenager, is nearby with a wheelbarrow. He takes out a rusty petrol can and approaches the cashier.*

Cashier Pump 12?

Shuttle Yeh.

Cashier £2.50?

Shuttle Yeh.

Cashier Is that old can safe?

Shuttle It's got a good lid.

Cashier It looks a bit rusty … (*Laughs.*) … like your wheelbarrow!

Shuttle Fiver?

Cashier Yeh fine. What are you doing with it?

Shuttle Nothing for you to worry about.

Cashier Really?

Shuttle Yeh.

Cashier Getting a new 'ped?

Shuttle I wish!

Cashier 'Cos like, you bought some yesterday …

Shuttle Someone nicked it.

Cashier Nicked it?

Shuttle Yeh.

Cashier I got to ask. You know.

Shuttle Next time I come, you'll see why.

Cashier (*Handing **Shuttle** the change.*) What do you mean?

Shuttle You'll see.

9

1 Embers

Cashier You like to be all secretive, don't you?

Shuttle Call it what you want. But you'll see. Are you on tomorrow?

Cashier Five till ten again.

Shuttle I'll come over.

Cashier Later.

Shuttle See you. (*He exits putting the can in the wheelbarrow.*)

Contemporary upbeat music preferably with 'fire' references fades up to lift the atmosphere and to introduce the photo-love sequence. If instrumental, it could underscore the scene.

2 Combustible material

This scene should be presented in the stilted style of a photo-love story.

Narrator (*A melodramatic voice-over.*) Stapping School. Mr Butcher's weekly detention. Our heroes …

Molly (*Dreaming.*) Ian … Ahhhh!

Ian (*Dreaming.*) Molly … Ahhhh!

Ian/Molly Dream date.

Narrator Fanning the flames of their desire.

Ian Molly! Top totty! Smokin'!

Molly Ian is hot as hell!

Narrator Incandescent teenage hearts.

Ian She has got a bit of a funny nose but …well, I'll just ignore it!

Butcher Molly Dukes?

Molly Yes, sir.

Butcher What are you doing?

Molly Sorry, sir?

2 Combustible Material

Butcher What were you doing?

Molly Nothing.

Butcher Nothing?

Molly Day-dreaming sir. Sorry, sir.

Butcher I'm surprised at you, Molly. Get on with your work, unless you want another detention tomorrow?

Molly Sorry sir.

Molly puts her head down and looks like she is working.

Ian I bet I know what she's dreaming about!

Butcher Ian Thorpe.

Ian (*Aside.*) Ian Thorpe! Just what I was thinking! (*To Mr Butcher.*) Sir?

Butcher You should be …

Ian/Molly/Butcher Thinking about your work!

Ian Sorry sir.

Ian puts his head down and looks like he is working.

Narrator That same night, in their separate homes …

Ian and Molly move to separate areas of the stage establishing their respective 'homes'.

Ian I want to text her … but I'm scared.

Molly I can't wait for him to make the first move. I know! I'll text him. I need to know what he thinks!

Narrator Eleven digits later … Ian's 'phone makes the message alert sound.

Ian A message? Who can this be from?

Molly/Ian Will u lite my fire? (*The text message could be projected onto a screen.*)

11

2 Combustible Material

Ian It could be a joke! I'll ignore it! No one makes a fool out of Ian Thorpe!

Narrator Next day at school …

Molly Hi Ian. (*Aside.*) Wonder if he got my message?

Ian Hi Moll. (*Aside.*) Was it her or not?

Molly Alright? (*Aside.*) He's being really off. It must be a 'No'.

Ian I'm fine! You alright?

Molly Yeh. I'm fine too!

Molly/Ian That's fine then!

Molly (*Aside.*) I'm getting out of here! Quick! Think up an excuse! (*To Ian.*) I've … I've got go to the loo … to erm … to … well … go to the loo! (*She makes to exit.*)

Ian No, Molly, wait a minute. Did you text me last night?

Molly (*Aside.*) I've got to be honest. I may never get this chance again to win my dream date! (*To Ian.*) Yes! (*Aside.*) I hope I'm sounding confident … (*To Ian.*) I've fancied you for ages.

Ian Either you're winding me up or you're … ?

Molly I'm not winding you up …

Ian So you …?

Molly Yeh.

Ian Seriously?

Molly Yeh!

Narrator Scorching … boiling … steaming … burning … Ian wants to rip his clothes off there and then!

Ian The offer still stands then?

Molly Tonight the moon is out … and so are my parents.

Narrator Mercury rising. Ian's thermometer is being tested to its limits!

2 Combustible Material

MOLLY So what do you say?

IAN What do I say?

MOLLY Will you go out with me?

IAN Fine.

MOLLY/IAN Well that's fine then!

MOLLY But I was joking!

IAN What?

MOLLY About my parents being out. They're sad and never go out.

IAN Sizzlers?

MOLLY Will we get in?

IAN Midge always does and he looks about eight!

NARRATOR The day passes slowly. Love on the backburner ...

IAN Molly ... Ahhh!

MOLLY Ian ... Ahhh!

NARRATOR Smouldering ... simmering.

MOLLY Ian ... ahhh!

IAN Molly ... ahhh!

NARRATOR They could hardly wait for ...

MOLLY/IAN ... fireworks at Sizzlers!

NARRATOR But nothing really happened!

IAN I don't know if she wants to go out with me.

MOLLY He won't make the first move.

IAN She seems a bit shy.

MOLLY He's scared.

IAN I don't want to be too pushy!

IAN/MOLLY (S)He's really fanciable!

2 Combustible Material

NARRATOR	One week later …
IAN	Cinema ….
MOLLY	Romantic comedy …
IAN	Don't normally go for them but …
MOLLY/IAN	It's brilliant!
NARRATOR	Two weeks pass … Half term holiday.
MOLLY	Shopping trip to London …
IAN	On our own …
MOLLY/IAN	Spend … spend … spend …
MOLLY	My birthday money …
IAN	And some of mine.
NARRATOR	The following day …
IAN	Crazy Golf.
MOLLY	Champion!
IAN	I let her win!
MOLLY	Didn't!
IAN	I could have beaten you easily!
MOLLY	But you didn't!
NARRATOR	The end of the half term holiday …
IAN	Sizzlers?
MOLLY	Cool!
NARRATOR	Someone will have to make a first move tonight … or it could all be off.
MOLLY	Dancing!
IAN	A bit nervous … so … go for some showing off!
MOLLY	Laughing!
IAN	Shouting over the music!

14

2 Combustible Material

Molly Getting closer.

Ian … warmer …

Molly … glowing …

Ian … smouldering …

Molly/Ian Teenage passion blazing …

Molly Lips …

Ian Press …

Molly On …

Ian Lips …

Molly/Ian Finally we kiss. But we're not showing you! That's private!

Narrator Ian even found he liked Molly's nose!

Ian Like it? I adore it! Your nose is the best, Molly …

Molly Gee … thanks a lot! Yours ain't too bad either.

Narrator Four weeks passed. Their fire sizzled …

Ian Swimming …

Molly Diving …

Ian Ducking …

Molly Play fighting …

Ian Flirting …

Molly/Ian Really getting to know each other.

Ian If you get my meaning!

Molly (*Warning.*) Ian!

Narrator Later that day Molly meets Ian's dad.

Molly Your dad's like, easier than mine. More relaxed.

Ian He's cool. 'So long as you're happy.' That's what he says.

2 Combustible Material

Molly (*Pause.*) Ian? There were pictures of your mum up in the house, but you never talk about her?

Ian Don't you know then?

Molly What?

Ian She died.

Molly I … I assumed that … well …

Ian Everyone does.

Molly I'm sorry.

Ian No need to be sorry … but … well … I thought everyone knew.

Molly I didn't.

Ian (*Smiling.*) Yeh … tough eh?

Molly Understatement. Was that why you came here?

Ian Dad wanted a fresh start. I wanted to stay but …

Molly You poor thing.

Ian She was real kind … (*Laughs.*) … most of the time.

Molly Do you mind talking about her?

Ian No. It's nice to … well, remember.

Molly How did she … what happened?

Ian Went in for a routine operation …. and … well … something went wrong … that was it really. My dad was like completely broken. It was scary seeing him like that when I was like upset too. And then my sister went right off the rails when we moved. She couldn't settle here and … well, dad blames himself.

Silence.

So when do I meet your mum and dad?

Molly I don't know …

Ian I want to meet them.

16

2 Combustible Material

Molly Dad'll just tease me. Not because it's you ... but ... well ...

Ian So what's the problem?

Molly Alright then. But not today.

Ian Soon?

Molly OK then. Soon.

Ian I want us to be serious, Moll.

Molly Can we change the subject?

Ian Is Louise coming tonight?

Molly Said she was.

Ian And Stueey?

Molly (*Disapproving.*) Yeh.

Ian He's alright. He's a laugh.

Molly He's a plonker!

Ian He's not as bad as you make out.

Molly Ian, there's no smoke without fire.

Ian So you wouldn't take him home then?

Molly I wouldn't ever go out with him!

Ian Nor would I!

Molly (*Laughs.*) I'm glad about that!

Ian So am I going to be allowed in your house?

Molly I thought we'd changed the subject.

Ian I've changed it back again. (*Molly gives Ian a disapproving look.*) Molly ... I want us to work.

Molly You're soppy you are.

Ian No one says that to me and gets away with it.

Molly Wanna bet? (*She puts her hand out.*)

2 Combustible Material

Ian Yeh.

Molly (*Running off.*) You'll have to catch me first! (*He chases after her.*)

Narrator Later that night dot, dot, dot!

3 Laying the Fuse

*It is evening mealtime in the Dukes' household. **Chris**, carrying a plate, and **Debbie** carrying two plates, are standing frozen by their dining table about to deliver the plates to the table. **Molly** is sitting down. The opening three lines are delivered from their frozen positions.*

Chris Mealtime.

Debbie Family time.

Molly Togetherness?

All Healthy salads ... Yum! (*They become animated simultaneously.*)

Chris (*Delivering a plate to Molly.*) You still going to the fair tonight Moll?

Molly Don't tell me you're coming too Dad!

Chris Wouldn't want to cramp your style love. (*He sits.*)

Debbie (*Delivering two plates, one to Chris and the other to her own place.*) Style? A quality from my side of the family! (*She sits.*)

Debbie Time to talk.

Chris Time to eat.

All Old fashioned family values!

Molly (*With forced enthusiasm.*) Yeh!

Debbie Eat.

Chris Converse.

Debbie Outlining plans for tomorrow ...

3 Laying the Fuse

Chris	Listening intently and contributing …
All	… politely.
Debbie	Talk about work … teaching.
Molly	Then …
Debbie	How was your day Chris?
Chris	You know that fire yesterday … well, arson …
Debbie	… up on Poachers' Hill …
Chris	Today there were two. One in the woods and another … could have been really serious … in the Heathwood Flats. The bin set alight.
Debbie	Related?
Chris	Maybe, yeh. We found these paper aeroplanes near each of the fires.
Molly	Weird.
Chris	Yeh, very.
Debbie	Sooner or later someone's going to get hurt … or worse. Then maybe they'll … (*Pausing.*) If you got hurt Chris … well … I don't know what I'd do.
Molly	What a cheerful conversation!
Chris	It's the real world Molly my love!
Debbie	The world in which we live.
Molly	Smile sweetly.
Chris	Eat.
Debbie	Converse.
Chris	All in a day's work for an overworked and underpaid fire-fighter!

Debbie and *Chris* laugh.

Molly	Smile sweetly again!
All	Eat.

3 Laying the Fuse

CHRIS   Lovely salad.

DEBBIE   Tomatoes from Grandad's garden.

CHRIS/DEBBIE   There's nothing like fresh tomatoes!

MOLLY   Smile sweetly. Not really concentrating … thinking about Ian … what he said today … that word 'serious'. What would he think to this? What will they think of him?

CHRIS   Alright, Molly?

MOLLY   Yeh. Fine.

DEBBIE   You don't seem very with it?

CHRIS   Don't you like Grandad's tomatoes?

MOLLY   To be honest, I can't tell the difference between them and the shop ones really.

DEBBIE   Can't you?

MOLLY   No.

DEBBIE   Oh I can. They're more … well …

MOLLY   (*Aside.*) Can't stop thinking about Ian … his mum …

CHRIS   Flavoursome.

MOLLY   (*Aside.*) … his sister …

DEBBIE   Yes. That's a good word.

MOLLY   (*Aside.*) … his life.

DEBBIE   They're more flavoursome.

DEBBIE/CHRIS   Flavoursome.

MOLLY   (*Aside.*) … I just can't stop thinking about Ian.

DEBBIE   Well they're a lot cheaper!

Chris and *Debbie* laugh.

MOLLY   Smile sweetly again. Eat.

ALL   Final mouthfuls on their way in …

3 Laying the Fuse

Chris Eat …

Debbie Eat …

Molly Eat … smile sweetly again.

All Finished.

They all put their cutlery down.

Molly What have we got for dessert?

Silence.

Hello! Is everything alright?

Chris Actually sweetheart … we've got something to say …

Molly What?

Debbie Some news.

Molly News? Not pregnant are you?

Silence.

You are?

Chris There's no easy way to tell you this, Molly, so I'll take the bull by the horns and …

Debbie We're going to be moving …

Molly *(Pause.)* What?

Chris I know it's not ideal for you Moll, but …

Molly Moving? Where?

Debbie We'll be getting a bigger, much nicer house.

Molly Am I going to have to change schools?

Chris We've given it a lot of thought.

Molly I'm not changing school!

Debbie You'll have to, love.

Molly No.

Debbie Dad's done well! He's …

3 Laying the Fuse

MOLLY I'm not changing school!

CHRIS Molly, we're moving to Muggington.

MOLLY Where the hell's that?

CHRIS Just outside Derby.

MOLLY Derby?

DEBBIE Dad's going to be a Station Officer.

MOLLY You didn't even talk to me about it!

DEBBIE We didn't want to worry you.

MOLLY Couldn't you have waited until I left school? Couldn't you have …?

CHRIS No. That's the blunt answer. Sometimes we have to put ourselves first. I'm sorry love, I know it's …

MOLLY You don't know anything!

DEBBIE You're not making this any easier.

MOLLY Do I look as though I care?

CHRIS Molly, listen. Why don't you … just go out … enjoy yourself …

MOLLY That's going to be easy now isn't it?

CHRIS … and we'll talk about it when you …

MOLLY It's a bit late for that! What is there to talk about?

DEBBIE What time are you meant to be meeting? Who are you going with? Louise?

CHRIS You two aren't going to that fair on your own are you?

MOLLY Ian and Stueey are coming.

CHRIS Well, be careful.

MOLLY What do you mean by that?

DEBBIE This Ian, we don't even know him.

MOLLY No point now you've done this?

22

DEBBIE	If he really likes you, moving won't make any difference.
MOLLY	It will! I hate you for this. I really hate you both.
	(Molly goes to exit.)
CHRIS	Do you want some money?
MOLLY	I've got my allowance. I'm not going to be bribed.
DEBBIE	What time will you be back?
MOLLY	I don't know!
CHRIS	Molly! We need to know what time you'll be back.
	***Molly** turns slowly to confront them.*
MOLLY	*(Measured.)* You never tell me anything, so why should I?
DEBBIE	Be back by ten Molly.
MOLLY	Whatever!
CHRIS	What's that supposed to mean?
MOLLY	It means … if I come back at all … I'll be back by ten! Alright? *(She leaves.)*
CHRIS	Molly, come back here! *(To **Debbie**.)* We can't let her go out like that.
DEBBIE	Give her some space Chris. She'll be alright.
CHRIS	I couldn't have done that worse if I'd tried.
DEBBIE	It was never going to be easy. As my mum used to say, we've made our bed …
CHRIS/DEBBIE	We've got to lie in it.

4 RAISING THE TEMPERATURE

***Shuttle** puts on his shoes. **Nan** stands over him.*

NAN	Goin' out William?
	***Shuttle** nods.*
	Where's you going?

4 Raising the Temperature

Silence.

Where to my love?

Silence.

Couldn't you just stay in? Just tonight?

Silence.

When'll you get back William?

Silence.

William? You knows how I worries. What are you going to be doin'?

SHUTTLE   Stuff.

NAN   You always says that.

Silence.

Never ending this 'stuff'.

SHUTTLE   You don't understand.

NAN   You won't do anything … you know?

Silence.

William?

SHUTTLE   I'm taking the wheelbarrow.

NAN   Is it working?

SHUTTLE   What do you mean?

NAN   The tyre … thought it was …

SHUTTLE   Fixed it two weeks ago, Nan. Is the shed locked?

NAN   You was there last. (*Pausing.*) Where you goin' with it?

SHUTTLE   Up Poachers. Then down to the school to see Slime.

NAN   Don't call him that William. (*Pausing.*) How long will you be?

SHUTTLE   Depends.

Nan	Shall I wait up?
Shuttle	Up to you.
Nan	Take your coat.
Shuttle	I'll be alright.
Nan	(*Passing Shuttle's coat to him.*) It's cold. Go on.
Shuttle	Don't want it.
Nan	I bought it for you. I thought it was …
Shuttle	(*Taking the coat.*) Alright.
Nan	You won't be back too late?
Shuttle	There's nothing to worry about Nan, especially tonight. I's got something goin' on to take my mind off it like. (*Pausing.*) I love you Nan. I don't mean to upset you.
Nan	I didn't think you'd remembered.
Shuttle	Nan, I remember every day. I just don't want to upset you by talking about it. (*Becoming upset.*) I'm embarrassing myself. I'd better be off.
Nan	Look after yourself my love and don't be back late eh?

Shuttle exits.

Silence.

Nan	(*Looking up to the sky.*) Jenny, why'd you have to up and leave us so suddenly like that? Why?

5 Sparks

*'Soppy' music plays as **Molly** and **Ian** enter, running towards each other in slow motion from either side of the stage and meeting in a passionate hug. They are both wearing hoodies under their coats.*

Molly	Ian!
Ian	Molly!
Molly	Ian!

5 Sparks

*Molly breaks down and cries in melodramatic fashion within **Ian's** hug.*

IAN What's the matter Moll?

Molly does not respond. Ian pulls her away from his body.

What's happened?

MOLLY My mum and dad are moving …

*In a stylised manner **Molly** and **Ian** turn to face the audience, momentarily, in mock horror, then return to their original position.*

They're taking me with them …

Molly and Ian repeat the stylised movement.

… to a small village on the outskirts of Derby.

The dialogue continues in a mock 'frightfully 1930's' English manner.

IAN Not … not Muggington surely?

MOLLY Golly gosh! How did you know that?

IAN Simple my sweet. The magic of theatre!

Molly and Ian both come out of role to clap and stamp in the fashion of a music hall entertainer and freeze momentarily before reverting to their roles.

(*Speaking with an air of undeserved seriousness.*) Actually, I heard your father say it in a previous scene!

MOLLY You did what?

IAN I know I shouldn't have been listening but … well it's too late now!

MOLLY So what are your views on my predicament?

IAN I have not yet formed such an opinion my darling.

5 Sparks

MOLLY   I hoped you may be thinking something along the lines of 'No one can hose our love down that easily?' or that 'Our love will continue to burn forever and a day'? Ian! I need you! I want you! I can't live without you!

IAN   But we've only known each other for …

MOLLY   Ian, you make me feel volcanic! I'm in danger of erupting!

IAN   Oh my word!

MOLLY   I love you!

IAN   I … well … I love you too!

Molly brings Ian's head to hers and kisses him. She forces his head back to talk to him. They revert to their normal voices.

MOLLY   Really?

IAN   Of course I do! It's just that … I'm … well … I'm a male, Molly … and males don't ever know what to say in these situations …

MOLLY   And even when they do it comes out all wrong and the female becomes upset and …

IAN   … that's how a lot of relationships come to …

MOLLY/IAN   … a very sticky end! (*To audience.*) But the introduction of a new character …

Stueey enters, also wearing a hoodie and coat.

MOLLY/IAN/STUEEY   Stueey!

IAN   Immediately causes friction … between Molly … and me.

STUEEY   And poses a crucial question.

MOLLY/IAN   How will our relationship be affected by the arrival of such a mischievous young lad?

MOLLY   Where's Lou?

IAN   Asks Molly …

5 Sparks

MOLLY ... Louise, being Stueey's girl-friend ...

IAN ... and Molly's best mate ...

MOLLY/IAN Neither of us are prepared for the explosion of temper from aforesaid Stueey ...

STUEEY (*Grossly overplayed.*) They said I can't see her anymore!

IAN What?

MOLLY Isn't she coming? I need to speak to her.

STUEEY (*Back to normal.*) She was going out. All dressed up posh. They said they don't want her associating with me. I mean, I only got excluded for swearing at a teacher ... and that was Butcher so that don't really count ... and then set off the fire alarm, which was dead funny 'cos I stood on the bridge watching everyone get soaked in the rain while the teachers tried to take the register. Morons!

6 Fanning the Flame

IAN (*To audience.*) Stueey was always getting into trouble. I'd only met him recently. I was kind of interested by him. I wondered, would he really do anything? So far the answer was ...

IAN/MOLLY/ STUEEY Yes! Yes! Yes!

STUEEY Like you daring me to fart loudly in assembly!

IAN But the assembly he chose, was like ... well, the very worst ...

STUEEY ... where everyone's silent, thinking about the soldiers who 'died for us'.

MOLLY And what was it you said to Miss Stonehart afterwards, Stueey?

STUEEY (*Innocently, as though to Miss Stonehart.*) I was making the sound of a machine-gun to help everyone imagine the war!

6 Fanning the Flame

IAN Everyone cracked up!

MOLLY (*To audience.*) Ian looks up to Stueey. He changes when Stueey's around. I don't like it, but what can I do?

IAN Molly, did you know Stueey's got this huge collection of lighters? Y' know, cigarette lighters?

STUEEY One hundred and seventy three, and I know where they all come from.

MOLLY Why do you collect them?

STUEEY I like them.

MOLLY Weird.

STUEEY Hang on a minute … can I just do a quick monologue?

IAN/MOLLY What?

STUEEY I just need to do a monologue. I won't be long.

IAN/MOLLY Do you always do this?

STUEEY Only if I need to. Don't you?

*Stueey moves to another part of the stage. **Ian** and **Molly** look on bemused.*

MOLLY He's weird!

STUEEY (*To audience.*) When I was a kid I remember someone telling me that if you rubbed two flints together you can make a spark. I remember trying it but it didn't work. Then someone showed me how, with a magnifying glass, you can burn little bits of paper or twigs or whatever. The brightness. It was glowing. Amazing! No matches. Just me, a magnifying glass and the sun. I even tried it on my hand. It really hurt! Everyone's tried that … haven't they?
(*He returns to **Ian** and **Molly**.*)

MOLLY Have you been kicked out for good now?

STUEEY (*Laughing.*) Nah … another final warning, but I don't care. I hate school. I hate teachers and the kids who go there …

6 Fanning the Flame

MOLLY/IAN Oy!

STUEEY Well most of 'em.

IAN Stueey?

STUEEY What?

IAN Do you know anything about these notes Butcher's been getting?

STUEEY Only they thought I was doing them.

IAN I got accused today.

STUEEY Thought you would.

MOLLY What's going on?

IAN Butcher's been getting threatening notes.

MOLLY How come I haven't heard anything?

STUEEY They're trying to keep it quiet.

MOLLY Who?

STUEEY/IAN Teachers.

MOLLY So what's been happening then?

IAN Butcher's been getting these notes …

STUEEY … threatening ones … left at school in his classroom … at night. They accused me. (*Grinning.*) Then someone said they'd seen you do it.

IAN You being serious? Who?

STUEEY Just heard that someone'd said.

IAN I didn't do it Molly. I had no reason to. Butcher's alright.

MOLLY You've always said you hate him.

IAN I didn't write the notes. I thought I'd been with you some of the evenings … but I hadn't.

MOLLY Do they still think it's you?

30

6 Fanning the Flame

Ian   Think so ... but it wasn't!

Molly   What do they say these notes?

Stueey   One said: 'Butcher ... Butcher ... I want to rip your big fat head off your big fat body ... and squeeze lemon juice into the open wound I've left on your big fat neck!'

Molly   That's sick!

Stueey   It's funny.

Ian   How do you know?

Stueey   They showed me!

Ian   Yeh?

Stueey   Listen, I've got an idea.

Ian/Molly   Ding! (*Intimating a lightbulb flash.*)

Stueey   (*Sarcastically.*) Very funny! Look, once we've been to the fair, we'll go up the school, and have a look round. Investigate like. We can clear both our names then.

Molly   I'm not so sure.

Stueey   You don't have to. Me an' Ian'll go on our own. It's up to you.

Ian   Come on Moll.

Molly   You'll only make matters worse.

Stueey   It's alright for you. You haven't been accused.

Ian   You never get accused of anything. I don't mean it nasty like but you don't, do you?

Molly   Maybe it's because I don't 'do' anything!

Ian   Nor do I.

Stueey   Why isn't anyone saying that about me then?

*Ian and **Molly** laugh. There is a pause.*

Stueey   Hey Molly ... what's all this about you moving to Muggington?

6 Fanning the Flame

Molly/Ian   How do you know about that?

Stueey   The magic of theatre!

Ian, Molly and Stueey clap and stamp music hall style.

What are you gonna to do?

Molly   I had planned to ask Lou tonight if I can live round hers … till I finish my GCSEs.

Stueey   With her dad?

Molly   Better than going to Muggington! I'm not moving and I told them!

Stueey   I bet that helped!

Molly   (*Sarcastically.*) Funny!

Ian   She just can't bear to be parted from me!

Molly   Depends if you're going to be a prat all night actually Ian!

Ian and Stueey freeze open-mouthed looking at Molly.

Well? Are you?

Ian   What's that meant to mean?

Stueey   Hey, are we still off to the fair or what?

Molly/Ian   Yup.

Stueey   I'd better own up then.

Ian   What?

Stueey   I ain't got no money!

Ian   What a surprise!

Molly   And actually Ian, I've only got … well, not much … maybe we'd better …

Ian   Look you two, don't worry. My Dad just got this new girl-friend and he wanted me out, if you know what I mean, so he gave me this. (*He shows them two £20 notes.*)

7 Fireworks at the Fair

Molly/Stueey Forty quid! What are we waiting for?

Molly/Ian/ The next scene …
Stueey

> *Ian, Molly and Stueey all do a 360° turn slowly in the same direction to simulate the change of location. Fairground music fades up.*

7 Fireworks at the fair

> *This scene should be performed at breakneck pace with the cast, working as a **Chorus**, physically representing all the fairground attractions as well as playing **Stall Holders** and punters*

All The fair! Yes!

Stall Holders Roll up … roll up come inside … tonight is just a quid a ride.

Stall Holder 1 Candyfloss, candyfloss.

> *Each of the **Stall Holders** continues to issue their announcement as the next one joins in, leading to a cacophonic montage of the fair.*

Stall Holder 2 Come inside and see the bearded lady … see the hair on this woman.

Stall Holder 3 Toffee apples … Toffee apples.

Stall Holder 4 Hook the duck, hook the duck.

> *The **Chorus** physically represent plastic ducks floating aimlessly but cheerily around a moat. Others hook them around the neck, which comically changes their expression!*

Stall Holder 5 Here's one for the sharpshooters. Five shots for a quid.

> *The **Chorus** physically represent the moving targets on a rifle range. One or more characters shoot on the command.*

All 1, 2, 3, fire!

7 Fireworks at the Fair

	*As the command 'Fire!' is given the range metamorphoses into a bar area for the **Hotdog Salesperson** to appear behind.*
STALL HOLDER 6	Hot dog! Hot dog! Get your hot dogs here!
STUEEY	Mmmm! Nice!
IAN/MOLLY/ STUEEY	Three hot dogs mate …
STALL HOLDER 6	(*With accompanying mime.*) Bun … sausage … sauce. (*Hands over the hot dogs.*)
IAN/MOLLY/ STUEEY	(*Collecting and eating their mimed hot dog in one choral mouthful.*) Mmmmm ! (*They belch chorally*)!
MOLLY	Roller-coaster!
	***Ian** and **Stueey** rush over onto the roller-coaster which is, again, represented physically by the **Chorus**.*
STUEEY	Come on then! Quick!
	*The action freezes. Everyone is motionless and silent. **Ian**, just behind **Stueey** who is about to get in, has second thoughts. He turns round slowly to look at **Molly**.*
MOLLY/IAN	One space only.
IAN	(*To **Molly** very seriously.*) Do you mind?
	*Pause. **Ian** freezes. Silence, amplifying the significance of **Ian's** choice. The **Chorus** point in slow motion at **Molly** to highlight her facial expression.*
MOLLY	(*Hesitantly.*) No. No you go. You go with Stueey, Ian.
	*A vocal heartbeat starts up as **Stueey** and **Ian** proceed to the roller-coaster leaving **Molly** behind. **Molly** stands alone.*
IAN	(*Immediately back to life.*) Cheers Moll.
	The pace picks up as they get on the roller-coaster. The locks click into position. The pace picks up immediately as they reconstruct the motion of the roller-coaster, left to right, backwards and forwards.

7 Fireworks at the Fair

Ian/Stueey Whooooah! Whooooah! Whooooah!

The roller-coaster morphs into a waltzer with the cast in threes or fours linking to spin round. **Molly** *rejoins* **Ian** *and* **Stueey's** *group where all playing the Waltzers chorally speak the following rhyme at an ever-increasing tempo.*

All Waltzer, waltzer round it goes, where will it stop nobody knows. Round and round and round it goes, where will it stop nobody knows.

Stueey (*Pointing.*) Look!

The **Chorus** *assemble to make a test-of-strength machine.*

Chorus (*As a test-of-strength machine.*) Test your strength. Win a lighter.

Stueey Ian? Win me a lighter mate.

Molly I'll do it if you want.

Stueey It's alright Moll. Ian'd be a much better bet.

Molly You reckon?

Stueey Yeh. (*To Ian.*) You're very quiet. Back me up Ian.

Ian Whatever!

Molly I'd beat either of you two goons any day.

Silence. **Ian** *does not respond.*

Ian, are you alright?

Ian Sorry. I just had a sudden thought about my mum. There's a fortune teller over there. She used to be kind of frightened of them. Just made me think.

Pause.

Stueey I tell you what, how much have you got left Thorpey?

Ian Three quid.

Stueey Just enough for two turns. So, you two love-birds take each other on. A challenge and whoever wins the lighter …

35

7 Fireworks at the Fair

Ian/Molly Yes?

Stueey Gives it to me. I ain't got that one!

Ian/Molly What's in it for us?

Stueey We'll see who's the strongest!

All (*Except Molly and Ian.*) Divide …

*Stueey steps between **Ian** and **Molly** forcing them apart.*

Stueey (*Confidently.*) … and rule.

***Ian** lifts a mimed hammer back behind his head. The **Chorus** make a soundscape to create the tension of the moment. As **Ian** hits it onto the pad he emits a loud shout.*

Ian Eurgh!

The little ball in the machine, represented by someone's fist, travels a little way up the tube with a dull vocal sound. Either side of the travelling fist, fingers wiggle denoting the lights flickering on as the ball travels upwards. The ball struggles to stay there then sadly returns down to its resting position.

Machine Wimp!

***Molly** steps up to the machine and with the support of the **Choral** soundscape effortlessly hits the hammer down on the pad. The ball rises rapidly, emitting excitable comic noises as it travels upwards, springs out of its container and does a celebration dance before finally returning joyfully to its resting position.*

Machine/Ian/Stueey Bloody hell Molly!

Ian/Stueey How the hell did you do that?

Molly The magic of theatre!

***Ian**, **Molly** and **Stueey** all clap and stamp music-hall style. The **machine** ceremoniously passes the lighter to Molly.*

7 Fireworks at the Fair

Stueey Can I have the lighter Molly?

Molly But I won it!

Ian Come on Molly! You did say!

Stueey Go on. Please.

Molly Here you are.

*The **machine** points at **Molly**, highlighting her action and emits a vocal heartbeat sound as **Molly** hands the lighter to **Stueey** in slow motion.*

Stueey Cheers Moll.

Ian What are we going to do now then?

*A sequence of freezes showing **Molly**, **Ian** and **Stueey** in different 'thinking' poses.*

Stueey Going to the school aren't we?

Silence.

Find out who's leaving those notes.

Molly I'm not sure.

Ian Molly!

Molly What?

Ian/Stueey Clear our names.

Molly How?

Stueey Private investigation.

Molly How do you know someone'll be there.

Ian If we don't look we won't find out.

Stueey Come on Molly … or wouldn't Daddy approve?

***Stueey** and **Ian** move as though to leave.*

Molly What?

Stueey Isn't he a pig?

7 Fireworks at the Fair

MOLLY Fire-fighter. Anyway I hate him!

*Over the next few lines the **test-of-strength machine** morphs in slow motion into a barrier separating **Molly** from **Ian** and **Stueey**.*

IAN So? You coming Molly?

MOLLY (*To audience.*) On any other day I'd tell'em both where to go, but today, possibly because of those four words …

STUEEY/IAN … 'or wouldn't Daddy approve?'

MOLLY I agree to go with them. (*She hesitantly opens the barrier and goes to follow **Ian** and **Stueey**.*)

BARRIER Molly?

***Molly** stops in her tracks and freezes looking at the barrier. The **Chorus** in the barrier sink to their knees with hands on heads.*

What are you doing?

MOLLY Maybe it's to get back at my dad. I don't know what it is, but whatever the reason, I join them in a …

MOLLY/IAN/STUEEY (*Adopting a still image and spoken to the audience in a cheesy American accent.*) … journey to our school.

MOLLY Which is so boring that we'll present a little play instead.

MOLLY/IAN/STUEEY How?

MOLLY The magic of theatre.

***Molly**, **Ian** and **Stueey** all clap and stamp à la old-fashioned entertainer.*

STUEEY A play that shall introduce to you …

MOLLY/IAN/STUEEY Shuttle …

IAN … who we are about to encounter.

Molly/Stueey	How do you know?
Ian	Premonition …
Molly/Stueey	Spooky!
Ian	Come on guys, let's do it before one of us dies!
Molly/Stueey	(*Adopting a freeze pointing the significance of this statement. Melodramatically.*) Is one of us about to die?
Ian	No, only joking. Let's just get on with it.
Molly/Ian/Stueey	(*In the manner of a game show host.*) Fantasy productions present …
Molly	The completely fabricated story of …
Molly/Ian/Stueey	William Weirdbeard …
Stueey	… known to us as …
Molly/Ian/Stueey	(*Climactically.*) Shuttle.
Stueey	Starring Stueey …
Molly/Ian	(*As **Stueey** enthusiastically dons a shawl.*) As Shuttle's Nan.

8 Meteor

This scene should be presented physically and imaginatively with the cast changing roles from human to inanimate objects frequently yet effortlessly.

Molly	Once upon a time, there lived, deep in a haunted forest (*The **Cast** become the spooky forest.*) a boy …
Ian/Shuttle	(*Displaying an awkward physical posture and a stiff wave.*) Greetings Earth beings.
Molly	…who's best friend was …
All	… his wheelbarrow.

One cast member becomes his wheelbarrow.

Molly	He lived in a ramshackle cottage with his ancient Nan.

Cast members become the cottage.

8 Meteor

Stueey/Nan (*As Shuttle's Nan in a clichéd witch voice.*) Pray, come ye no closer. Those who cross my boundary shall never return.

Molly Many believed that Shuttle's Nan had special powers.

Nan And those who do not shall have thunderbolts hurled at them!

Nan casts her hand forward and a loud pyrotechnic explosion and flash is cued.

Ian She could read people's fortunes like … a duck to water!

Nan (*Approaching **Molly** and taking her hand.*) Child, I see a line saying your family will move … move to … (*Overplaying the struggle to find the name and then stating it melodramatically and climactically.*) … to Muggington!

Molly/Ian Well impressive!

Nan But child, you will not be accompanying them …

Molly Too right I won't!

Nan You will be … (*Concerned she pushes **Molly's** hand away.*)

Molly Take it easy old woman!

Nan You will be … elsewhere.

Pause.

Ian Some say that she's not his real Nan.

Molly …but that he was loaned to the old woman while his alien parents took time out to record an …

Ian/Molly … interplanetary Rap Opera.

Molly But he did have one special talent …

All This bit is true actually.

Molly … he created giant sculptures in the grounds of our school.

*The **Cast** are sculpted into position by **Ian** as Shuttle.*

8 Meteor

Ian They were great …

Stueey … great fun to knock down.

Ian Once he made this really rude one.

Make the most of the opportunity to make this frozen image for comic effect!

Stueey We didn't knock that one down.

Ian/Stueey But the teachers did.

***Molly**, **Ian** and **Stueey** all laugh.*

Molly He was always alone.

Ian … and built himself a hideout, high on Poachers' Hill.

Molly To gaze at the stars. And this is how we came to call him …

All Shuttle.

Molly Scanning the skies for the UFO to arrive …

Ian … with the news that his parents had completed the interplanetary Rap Opera.

Molly And that he could return to his alien family …

Ian The end!

All Ahhh!

Ian That was good that.

Molly Like Edward Scissorhands without the scissors.

Stueey Sssssh.

Ian/Molly What?

Stueey Look!

Ian/Molly What?

Stueey Look! There! In the petrol station!

Ian/Molly Shuttle!

Molly Ian, your premonition?

9 Ignition

Ian	My powers are pretty amazing eh?
Molly/Stueey	Does this also mean one of us will die?
Ian	(*Laughing.*) We'll soon find out, but you know what I can't work out? Well, I don't think any of us can …
All	…what is Shuttle doing in a petrol station?

They freeze and the action cuts to the kiosk at a petrol station.

9 Ignition

*A **Cashier** stands at a till in a petrol station kiosk. **Shuttle**, an individualistic teenager, is nearby with a wheelbarrow. He takes out a rusty petrol can and approaches the cashier.*

Cashier	Pump 12?
Shuttle	Yeh.
Cashier	£2.50?
Shuttle	Yeh.
Cashier	Is that old can safe?
Shuttle	It's got a good lid.
Cashier	It looks a bit rusty …. (*Laughs.*) … like your wheelbarrow!
Shuttle	Fiver?
Cashier	Yeh fine. What are you doing with it?
Shuttle	Nothing for you to worry about.
Cashier	Really?
Shuttle	Yeh.
Cashier	Getting a new 'ped?
Shuttle	I wish!
Cashier	'Cos like … you bought some yesterday …
Shuttle	Someone nicked it.

CASHIER	Nicked it?
SHUTTLE	Yeh.
CASHIER	I got to ask. You know.
SHUTTLE	Next time I come, you'll see why.
CASHIER	(*Handing* **Shuttle** *the change.*) What do you mean?
SHUTTLE	You'll see.
CASHIER	You like to be all secretive don't you?
SHUTTLE	Call it what you want. But you'll see. Are you on tomorrow?
CASHIER	Five till ten again.
SHUTTLE	I'll come over.
CASHIER	Later.
SHUTTLE	See you. (*He exits putting the can in the wheelbarrow.*)

10 THE TINDERBOX

IAN/MOLLY	What is Shuttle doing at a petrol station?
STUEEY	Buying petrol I suppose.
IAN/MOLLY	Why?
STUEEY	I don't know!
MOLLY	Maybe something really big's going to happen?
STUEEY	Like what? Come on Ian, with your super psychic powers!
IAN	Unfortunately my powers have mysteriously deserted me.
MOLLY/STUEEY	How bloody inconvenient!
STUEEY	You two, can you just wait there a moment. I need to do another monologue.
MOLLY/IAN	So soon?

10 The Tinderbox

Stueey I won't be long but don't go, alright? (*He moves to the front of the stage and addresses the audience.*) This wasn't the first time that Shuttle had bought petrol. I don't quite know what he's up to, but yesterday, during the day, I was bored, so I thought I'd go up to Shuttle's hideout, the one on Poachers' Hill, just to look, I suppose. But I found this can. A can of petrol like, kind of hidden, dug into the ground. It was too tempting. You should have seen his den when it was alight! Glowing it was. Amazing!

Molly/Ian (*Shouting over to **Stueey**.*) Come on Stueey! Hurry up!

Stueey (*Shouting back.*) I'm being as quick as I can!

Molly/Ian Just hurry!

Stueey (*With a sense of urgency to complete the story.*) The fire brigade came. Maybe Molly's dad was there. No one saw me. Well, I don't think they did. Not even Shuttle when he came back … hah … (*Grinning.*) …you should have seen his face! (*Stueey returns to Molly and Ian.*)

Ian You done now?

Stueey Yeh.

Ian Come on or school'll've closed. Evening classes finish about 9.30.

Stueey Sports bit stays open till loads later.

Molly Looks like we're not the only ones.

Ian What do you mean?

Molly Look! Shuttle. With his little wheelbarrow. You don't think it could be him writing the notes?

Ian Shuttle?

Stueey It ain't him. I know it ain't.

Molly What's Shuttle gonna do with that petrol eh? (*Pausing.*) Oh what? I've just realised. Listen you two! My dad was

10 The Tinderbox

talking tonight. He said there was this fire up Poachers' Hill, near Shuttle's hideout yesterday ... and another today or something. It may even have been ... come on you two ... we've got to find out what he's up to!

Stueey What else did he say?

Molly He seemed to think they were being set on purpose.

Stueey What? Arson?

Molly Yeh. Come on you two. We've got to follow him!

Ian Molly, can't we skip the journey? I want to see what's going to happen.

Stueey How?

Ian/Molly The magic of theatre!

Ian, Molly and Stueey all clap and stamp music hall style.

Stueey That's well clever you two! Right outside the School Gates with no effort whatsoever ... like ... I don't know ... Peter Pan. And a great view of Butcher's window.

Molly Oy! You two! Look! Look at that!

Ian/Stueey What?

Molly It's Shuttle.

Ian What's he doing?

Stueey And Slime.

Ian What? Slime the caretaker?

Molly (*Correcting.*) Site Supervisor.

Stueey Did you know he and Shuttle are brothers?

Ian You're kidding?

Stueey Serious.

Ian I thought Shuttle was ...

Stueey What're they doing?

10 The Tinderbox

MOLLY Taking a whole load of stuff in his little wheelbarrow round by the bins.

STUEEY What's he up to then?

IAN Could be anything.

MOLLY They're going to set the bin alight.

STUEEY They won't. It'd be seen. It's too open round there.

IAN Where've they gone?

MOLLY Don't know!

STUEEY Can't you magic us round the other side of the building so that we can see?

IAN/MOLLY Don't be stupid!

STUEEY You did it a minute ago.

IAN Stueey, you're crazy mate!

MOLLY We could walk round.

STUEEY They'll be gone by then.

IAN Where?

STUEEY (*Becoming increasingly agitated.*) Come on you did it a minute ago ... by magic ... magic of theatre ... come on!

MOLLY Look!

IAN/STUEEY What?

MOLLY (*Pointing.*) Butcher's room!

IAN What? (*Gasps.*) Who is it?

STUEEY Shuttle and Slime wouldn't've had time to get up there. That can mean one thing and one thing only!

IAN/STUEEY Someone else is in there.

STUEEY And they could be leaving a note for Butcher.

IAN/STUEEY Come on we've got to get in there.

11 Arson About?

Molly But that bit of the school is always locked this late.
Stueey I can find a way in.
Molly Are you sure?
Stueey Certain. Come on, follow me.
Molly Whoever it was has gone now.
Ian We've got to get the note! We've got to …
Molly But what about Shuttle?
Stueey/Ian What about him?
Stueey Come on Molly do some of your magic of theatre stuff. I know you can!
Ian Stueey?
Molly I'll give it a go. Hold tight!

Molly, Ian and Stueey join together and with similarities to the way the roller-coaster ride was presented.

Ian Whooo! This is so cool!
Stueey Yeh! Way better than that roller-coaster!
Molly By the magic of theatre we find ourselves in the middle of a ground floor classroom.
Stueey Only a flight of stairs away from …
Stueey/Ian Butcher's room.
Stueey Brilliant Molly! I want to learn how to do that. It could come in well handy!

11 Arson About?

Ian, Stueey and Molly are crouched down, hiding. They have pulled their hoods up. The conversation is in hushed whispers.

Molly I can't believe I'm doing this.
Stueey Sssh!
Molly Goon!

11 Arson About?

Stueey Someone's out there.

Ian Who?

Stueey How do I know?

Silence.

Ian They're leaving.

Molly Thank God for that!

Stueey Whoever it is did us a favour by leaving that fire door open downstairs!

Molly I'm not entirely sure about all this.

Stueey (*Imitating.*) 'I'm not entirely sure ...' Relax you didn't have to come!

Molly I was hardly going to stay outside, on my own in the dark, was I?

Stueey Well now you're here. Just chill, 'cos I'm off to Butcher's room. See if there's anything there ... like a note. (*To **Ian**.*) You coming?

Ian Yeh OK.

Molly Well I'm not moving!

Ian Molly!

Stueey Stay here then. Both of you.

Ian Go on Moll.

Molly I'm not moving!

Stueey You stay with her. Alright?

Ian OK then.

Stueey But keep quiet and ... (*Smiling.*) ... don't get up to anything while I'm away!

Ian How're you gonna get into his room?

Stueey Easy! (*He exits.*)

Silence.

11 Arson About?

MOLLY Why the hell have I got myself involved in this? What if he gets caught? What if we get caught? How long's he gonna be?

IAN How do I know?

Pause.

MOLLY I don't trust him.

IAN He's alright!

MOLLY Ian, we've broken into a school. Our school!

IAN It'll be worth it if we find something!

MOLLY 'If' Ian! 'If!'

Pause.

Do you know what I think?

IAN Go on.

MOLLY You're so gullible.

IAN What?

MOLLY It's all a charade.

IAN Speak in English Molly! All your big words. What are you trying to say?

MOLLY Stueey's written those notes to Butcher. I'm sure of it. He's broken in here before to put them there. You can tell. He's way too calm about everything and I reckon that's what he's gone to do now.

IAN What?

MOLLY To plant another note there.

IAN But he asked us to go with him. We could easily have said yeh, then we'd've seen him do it.

MOLLY He didn't exactly ask.

IAN You're just like a bloody teacher. That's what they'd say. You're the only reason I didn't go with him! He's not like that. He's a mate, he's …

49

11 Arson About?

Molly   Ian! He's always in trouble and you know he is!

Ian   There are reasons.

Molly   Ian! I want to go.

Ian   I'm staying. I can't do that to him.

Molly   But you'll do this to me.

Ian   (*Confused.*) What?

Molly is suddenly distracted by a bang outside the door.

Molly   (*Whispering to Ian.*) What's that?

Ian   (*Whispering.*) Shit!

Silence.

Molly   (*Whispering.*) Did you hear something?

Ian   (*Whispering.*) Yeh. We're gonna get done.

Molly   (*Whispering.*) And Stueey's not here … why the …

Ian   (*Whispering.*) I don't believe this.

Ian creeps towards the door.

Molly   Where are you going?

Ian   Stay there.

Molly   (*Whispering.*) No … Ian.

Ian … don't … please … just stay down.

Ian   (*Getting up. Whispering.*) Can't see anything.

Molly   (*Whispering.*) Get down!

Ian   (*Whispering.*) Keep real quiet. I'm going to open the door.

*As the door is being opened **Stueey** springs in loudly. He is wearing gloves.*

Stueey   Surprise!

11 Arson About?

Molly You big goon!

Stueey I heard my name.

Molly You bloody goon Stueey!

Stueey (*Talking at a normal volume.*) What were you saying?

Ian What the hell are you doing coming back and scaring us like that?

Stueey Don't answer my question.

Molly Will both of you bloody shut up?

Stueey No need to worry! No one's around. I checked the corridor.

Molly Please Stueey! Keep it down.

Ian moves to stand upright and also starts speaking more loudly.

Ian So, did you get into Butcher's room?

Stueey Yup. And look what I got!

Stueey illuminates his lighter and puts the note in front of it. Molly and Ian gently take hold of it.

All (*Reading.*) 'Butcher, Butcher burning bright … look around you'll see your kids alight.'

Molly Stueey, put the lighter out. You'll be seen!

Stueey No need to panic Molly! (*He shuts off the lighter.*) I certainly ain't!

Molly I've just thought. (*Pausing.*) You didn't have time to get that note and bring it back.

Ian Moll!

Stueey I did. It was stuck on Butcher's window. You know, of his door.

Molly Why didn't you leave it there?

Stueey What good would that've done?

11 Arson About?

Molly   Well now you've got it, let's go!

Stueey   Not yet. I ain't finished. In fact I've only just begun.

Molly   Well I'm off.

Stueey walks over to pick up some files.

Stueey   (*To **Molly**.*) Go on then.

Ian   (*To **Stueey**.*) What're you doing Stueey?

Molly   Ian?

Stueey   Nothing. (*He picks up a file of papers and empties them on the floor.*)

Molly   Stop it Stueey!

Stueey   (*Mimicking.*) 'Stop it!' (*He gets more papers and tips them over the floor.*)

Ian   (*To **Stueey**.*) What are you doing?

Stueey   Having a laugh. They blame me for everything. Now here's something else for them to have a go at me for! (*He gives the paper a kick. He gets another file from the room and hurls it in the air.*)

Molly   (*Trying to intervene physically.*) That's enough Stueey.

Stueey   (*Pushing her away hard.*) Stressed Molly?

Ian   Come on Stueey.

Stueey   (*Grinning.*) I'm just starting to enjoy myself!

Ian   Now we've got the note shouldn't we …

Stueey   (*Calm but assured.*) If you go Ian I'll shout. I'll shout loud to make sure we get caught. I don't care … but I think you will!

Molly   Come on Stueey. Ian said we'd go if you found something.

Stueey   Did you Ian?

Ian   Not exactly.

11 Arson About?

Molly You did!

Stueey Well, I'm not ready yet!

Molly People can see from the road. We know that, 'cos we could!

Stueey (*Taunting.*) You don't have to stay Molly. Does she Ian? Here Ian, grab one of these! (*He hands Ian a piece of paper from the floor.*) Make a paper aeroplane.

Molly What … what did you say?

Stueey and *Ian* continue making paper aeroplanes.

Stueey I told Ian to make a paper aeroplane. Got a problem with that have we Molly?

Molly (*Alarmed.*) A paper aeroplane … this is stupid … really stupid! I'm going! Coming Ian?

Ian In a moment.

Molly Ian! Seriously!

Stueey In a minute!

Molly You won't even see them in the dark so what's the point?

Stueey Who says we won't. (*He gets out his lighter.*)

Molly What are you doing?

Stueey Gonna light them … (*He ignites the lighter.*)

Ian Hey, cool! Then we can see them!

Stueey Just the tips.

Stueey/Ian Wicked!

Molly Ian! I didn't think you were so stupid. We're finished and I'm not bullshitting!

Ian Wait Molly! I just want to see what happens!

Molly No! I'm off! (*Makes to exit.*)

Ian Molly, wait … only a minute!

11 Arson About?

Molly I'm out of here!

Ian OK then? I'm coming. (*Makes to exit.*)

Stueey So you don't want to know who did the notes then Ian?

Ian What?

Molly I'm not waiting.

Stueey Come on mate ... and I'll tell you who grassed you up.

Ian You said you didn't know.

Stueey I was lying.

Molly I don't know why you listen to him but tonight I've found out that you do ... and that's ... you're sad ... you're sad ... well sad. You're not who I thought you were at all!

Stueey If you stay here Ian, we'll have a laugh. Set some of these off and I will, I'll tell you who said they saw you!

Molly You're like kids you two, playing with fire. So you stay ... stay and play with your paper aeroplanes! And Ian, I hope you get your little nugget of information ... and it's worth it!

Ian Molly wait!

Molly I'm going on my own! You stay here!

Ian makes as though to follow. Molly turns on him.

I mean it!

Molly pushes Ian towards Stueey and leaves them both.

Ian Molly?

Stueey That told you mate!

Ian Stupid bitch!

Stueey (*Calling after Molly.*) Don't know why he fancied you anyway ... your nose don't even match your face!

11 Arson About?

Stueey and *Ian* laugh out loud. The laughter carries on as a sound effect with echo during which *Stueey* and *Ian* leave the stage and the *Chorus* assemble around *Molly*. The lights pick them out in silhouette. All their lines are accompanied by stylised movements to emphasise *Molly*'s fright and isolation.

Chorus 1 Ian's laugh cremates that young love's dream … her heart yells …

Molly (*Crying out very loud.*) I hate Ian … I hate him!

Chorus 2 Billowing derisory sound … suffocating her mind …

All (*Taunting challenge.*) Find your way through this.

Chorus 1 And though she might have wished to dish the dirt …

Chorus 3 Molly didn't have the guile to grass … or scream …

Chorus 2 No time to dream of being in the warm surroundings of her home.

The pace quickens and becomes increasingly more threatening.

Chorus 1 Just fear …

Chorus 3 And panic.

Chorus 2 And fear and panic.

Chorus 1 And panic and fear …

All … and panic!

Molly What do I do now?

Chorus 2 Got to go back.

Molly Can't!

Chorus 2 Got to!

Molly I'll look so stupid!

Chorus 1 Then leave.

Molly Which way?

11 Arson About?

Chorus 3 You choose!

Molly This way.

Chorus 2 (*Forming a barrier echoing the fairground scene.*) No!

Molly This way.

Chorus 3 (*Forming another barrier.*) No!

Molly So where?

All (*Surrounding **Molly**.*) You choose!

Molly This way! (*She breaks through.*)

Chorus 1 Footsteps.

Chorus 2 Faster.

Chorus 3 Fleeing.

All 3 Disaster.

Molly Faster.

All 3 Disaster!

Molly Faster!

All/Molly Disaster!

Molly Nightmare! I hear keys. Locking or … or unlocking a door somewhere … someone's approaching … someone coming to investigate.

All 3 You'll have to go back!

Molly Can't.

All 3 You'll have to!

Chorus 1 If you don't want to be caught.

Chorus 2 How'll you explain being here?

Chorus 3 What'll your Mum and Dad say?

Chorus 2 You can't grass the others up.

Suddenly more slowly and more threatening.

11 Arson About?

All	You'll have to take the blame!
Molly	(*Deep breathing. Hesitantly.*) Nearby ... there's an area ... a place where we leave our coats and bags ...
Chorus 3	You could hide there?
Chorus 2	But if the light goes on you'll be seen.
Molly	A classroom! One might be unlocked? Stueey said he could get in! Butcher's classroom. Where is it?
Chorus 2	What if someone comes?
Molly	Don't care! Got to try!
Chorus 1	Try this one ... (*Barring her entry.*)
Chorus 2	Or this? (*Barring her entry.*)
Chorus 3	This one's open.

Molly goes through Chorus 3 and squats low on the floor.

Molly	Oh my God!
Chorus 1	Hold your breath!
Chorus 2	Keep quiet!
Chorus 3	(*Taunting.*) Someone's seen you.
Molly	I wait.
Chorus 3	(*Taunting.*) Someone's seen you.
Molly	Footsteps approach.
Chorus 3	(*Taunting.*) Someone's definitely seen you.
Molly	Why aren't the lights going on?
Chorus 2	A key goes in the lock and ...
Chorus 1	It turns!
All 3	Locked ...
All 3/Molly	Locked in!

11 Arson About?

Chorus 2 Footsteps fade.

Chorus 1 Time passes.

Molly I can't stay here doing nothing!

All 3 What are you going to do?

Molly Go back and find Ian?

All 3 Gone by now.

Chorus 1 Locked in.

Chorus 2 Smash the window!

All 3 You'll have to smash the window!

Molly (*Trying to stand up. The **Chorus** restrict her movement.*) I can't!

All 3 Butcher, Butcher burning bright …

Molly I can't smash it.

All 3 Butcher, Butcher burning bright …

Molly I can't bloody smash it.

All 3 Stop!

Molly Why?

All 3 What's that smell?

Molly Burning.

All 3 Butcher, Butcher burning bright …

Molly Shut up and let me out!

*Molly struggles but the **Chorus** hold on to her.*

All 3 Look around you'll see your kids alight.

Molly No! His kids! Anything, but not me!

All 3 Butcher, Butcher …

Chorus 1 Fire alarm …

Chorus 2 Loud.

11 Arson About?

Chorus 3 Ringing.

Molly The door starts to give …

Chorus 1 An explosion!

Chorus 2 The Science labs.

Molly Let me out!

All 3 (*Suddenly encouraging her.*) Come on Molly you can do it!

Molly Done it! I'm out.

All 3 Well done Molly!

Chorus 1 Look what's here to greet you.

Molly Smoke …

All 3 Billowing smoke …

Molly Suffocating …

All 3 Choking …

Molly Suffocating.

All 3/Molly Then everything goes completely blank. Completely blank.

> *In silence* **Chorus 1** *moves* **Molly** *to a different part of the stage, controlling her movement as if she is a puppet. From this point on* **Molly** *becomes her own spirit watching the remainder of the play. As she is walked away* **Chorus 2** *and* **3** *take Molly's coat and formally lay it down to represent the position of her physical body. The* **Chorus** *stand looking out to the audience.*

All 3 Butcher, Butcher Burning Bright … look around.

> *The* **Chorus** *turn in slow motion to look at* **Molly's** *coat and freeze.*

(*Pause.*) … you'll see your kids alight.

They exit.

12 THE SMOKES CLEARS

MOLLY Shit scared! I was more scared than a really scared thing being scared by a scary monster with big teeth and hand-grenade claws! There's been a fire. That much is obvious. Stueey ... the paper aeroplanes ... Shuttle ... the petrol ... were they in it together? What's happened to Ian? I'm so scared! What the hell has happened?

Shouting in the distance ... and then ... I see ... well weird ... I see a body slumped in the corridor ... and it's really freaking me right out! There's a powerful smell of smoke ... but that's all ... it doesn't affect my breathing. A couple of fire-fighters pile in with their breathing apparatus and torches which focus on the body. They don't see me, and I don't know whether to shout or hide.

I stand back ... well back ... I don't want to be seen. They crouch over the body ... and then I see the face ... not burnt ... not damaged in any way. And realise that I know that face. It's not Ian, not Stueey, not Slime, not Shuttle and definitely not Butcher. I know this face intimately. This is well scary ... 'cos ... I realise that ... that ... It's so creepy ... (*Laughs.*) ... spooky ... I'm a ... and I'm well spooked out!

Then ... (*Becoming concerned at her lack of control.*) ... that scene fades and I find myself being transported ... not the magic of theatre ... no ... this is different ... shrieked through time and space. Right into my front room ...

Chris *is on the 'phone,* **Debbie** *is sitting unworried.*

My front room in my house. My mum, and my dad?

CHRIS (*Putting the 'phone down.*) That was Ian ... they've had a row, and Moll's walked off. He wanted to know if she was here.

DEBBIE She's probably gone round Louise's.

CHRIS It's nearly ten. Do you want to 'phone?

60

12 The Smoke Clears

Debbie   Not now ... she isn't due back for another five or so minutes ... we can't go 'phoning until she's late.

Pause.

Chris   Do you want a cup of tea?

Debbie   (*Laughing.*) No, and you shouldn't either. It'll only make you wee in the middle of the night and then you'll wake me up and I'll never get back to sleep again.

Chris   (*Laughs.*) Suppose.

Pause.

Do you really think we're doing the right thing? The move?

Debbie   You know I do. It's exciting ...

Chris   Yeh, but Molly ...

Debbie   She'll be fine.

Molly   Will I?

Chris   I hope she will.

Debbie   Trust me.

Chris   We could have left it for ... I don't know ... until she's eighteen.

Debbie   Four years? We can't put our lives on hold. You know what it's like these days. You'll be too old before long.

Chris   Who are you calling too old?

Debbie   You know what I mean.

Chris   Yeh.

Debbie   Don't go on beating yourself up about it Chris. It won't do you any good.

Chris   I don't like seeing her upset.

Debbie   This weekend we'll go up house hunting.

Chris   I want Moll to come with us.

12 The Smoke Clears

DEBBIE We'll see.

CHRIS We can make it nice for her. Stay in a hotel ... the one I stayed in when I went up for the interview ... it's lovely ... really posh!

DEBBIE Expensive though.

CHRIS It's only money! Anyway it'll be worth it ... indoor pool and everything.

DEBBIE She'll love that ... yeh go for it!

CHRIS I'll book it tomorrow.

MOLLY I won't be there though Mum ... I can't make it.

The doorbell rings.

DEBBIE That'll be her ...

MOLLY It can't be.

CHRIS What's wrong with her key?

DEBBIE She can see we're up.

CHRIS She'd better not have lost it again!

***Debbie** exits.*

MOLLY It can't be me ...

CHRIS (*Not looking in **Molly's** direction.*) I'm sorry Molly.

MOLLY Dad can you see me?

CHRIS (*Still not catching **Molly's** eye.*) I didn't do this to make life difficult. Perhaps we all need to sleep on it.

MOLLY Dad, it's me who's sorry! I don't quite know what's happened but ... well I don't want you to be angry with me. What's happened is nothing to do with ...

***Debbie** returns with **DC Ford**.*

DEBBIE Chris? It's ... it's someone from the police station.

MOLLY I don't want to be here for this!

CHRIS The police?

12 The Smoke Clears

Molly Please ... how do I get out of here! Let me out!

Chris Anxiety.

DC Ford Hello, my name is Martin Ford. I'm a Family Liaison Officer from Faversham police station. Can we sit down for a moment? I need to speak to you about your daughter Molly.

Debbie Worry.

DC Ford Preparing the way ...

Molly rushes over to her dad who remains oblivious of her.

Molly I'm so sorry!

Chris Predicting.

Debbie Mind racing.

Chris Molly?

Molly Dad ... you've got to be brave.

Debbie Something's happened to Molly!

Chris/Debbie What's she done?

DC Ford Gentle words.

Debbie Fearing the worst.

Chris Sensing grave, grave news.

Molly (*Going to Debbie.*) Please ... I don't want you to know!

Chris Not daring to imagine.

Chris/Debbie What the bloody hell's happened to her?

DC Ford Still not saying.

Chris Desperate.

Debbie Petrified.

Chris Disbelieving.

12 The Smoke Clears

DC Ford   Fire.

Chris/Debbie   Fire?

DC Ford   Body.

Chris/Debbie   A young girl's body?

Molly   But I'm here! Look! It's a dream … it has to be a dream!

Chris   It can't be Moll! It can't be! She was at the fair!

DC Ford   The evidence suggests from documentation found on the body that it … that it was Molly.

Debbie   What?

Chris   You must've got it wrong.

DC Ford   We found some ID in the pocket of her jacket.

Debbie   And this was at the school?

Chris   She had no reason to be at the school.

Debbie   Inside the school?

DC Ford   We found a purse.

Chris   She must've had it stolen …

Molly   Don't Dad!

Debbie   … at the fair.

Molly   I'm so sorry to put you both through this!

Chris   Someone must have stolen her purse. Come on, even I can work that one out! She'll be home any minute, you'll see.

Molly   I'd do anything to change what happened … anything! Please! Just let me out of here!

DC Ford   What time did she say she'd be back?

Pause. **Chris** *and* **Debbie** *look at one another.*

Debbie   Ten o'clock.

12 The Smoke Clears

Chris She went to the fair. I mean she actually got there. We know that for sure. Her boy-friend 'phoned a little minute ago, he told us.

DC Ford Her boy-friend? We'll need to speak to him. What's his name?

Chris Ian …

Debbie …Ian Thorpe.

DC Ford You said he 'phoned. When was that?

Chris A few minutes ago. Literally a few … They'd had a row. He 'phoned to ask if she'd come back here. She wouldn't've gone to the school. I mean it doesn't make any sense!

Debbie Why would she?

Chris Was anyone else hurt in this fire?

DC Ford We're not certain at the moment. There were evening classes on. Everyone was evacuated.

Chris And it was big … you know, serious?

DC Ford It happened in an area of the school that was locked off.

Chris How come … this girl … was there then?

DC Ford We don't know. That's what we'll try to find out.

Chris Do you think this girl you've found actually did it? Actually set the fire?

DC Ford It's too early to tell.

Chris It just can't be Molly!

Silence.

Debbie You'll be wanting us to do an identification?

Chris Debbie?

DC Ford We will, yes, but, let's do that tomorrow morning after we've found out more. I'll find another officer to sit

13 The Smoke Clears

with you. In the meantime we'll try to establish exactly what has happened. Here's my mobile number. (*He hands* **Chris** *a card.*) Ring me if you want to ask any questions and I'll let you know immediately if I hear anything else.

As he turns **Chris** *and* **Debbie** *move towards him.*

You stay there. I'll let myself out. (*He exits.*)

Pause.

CHRIS There's some massive mistake been made here. It's got to be please! (*He breaks down.*) It's got to be a mistake. Molly … my Molly!

*Chris is comforted by **Debbie**, who also begins to cry. **Molly** tries to get close to **Chris** then **Debbie**. Something stops her.*

MOLLY You can't hear me can you? I want to talk to you! I want you to hold me … hold me please!

And then, I travel without seeming to move whatsoever or having any control over where I go, the scenery around me changes. An image of an interior of a kind of warehouse emerges in front of me … and there they are, Ian and Stueey, tussling on the floor.

13 BURNT FINGERS

***Stueey** is sitting on **Ian** pinning him to the floor and holding him roughly by the neck.*

STUEEY You'd better keep your mouth shut?

IAN Get off!

STUEEY We didn't do nothing. Right?

IAN Stueey get off!

STUEEY Say it!

IAN What about Molly?

STUEEY (*Applying increased physical pressure.*) Say it!

13 Burnt Fingers

Ian OK then. Just let go!

Stueey Say it!

Ian What?

Stueey You won't squeal!

Ian I won't!

Stueey You'd better not!

Molly Stueey ... leave him!

Ian (*Stueey gives one last twist to **Ian's** arm.*) Ow!

Stueey (*Getting off and releasing **Ian**.*) You're dead if you say anything! I mean it! We don't admit to nothing. We ain't done nothing, so they can't pin nothing on us!

Ian We were there!

Stueey You were the one who went off on your own.

Ian Looking for Molly ...

Stueey Took long enough.

Ian I didn't have the lighter.

Stueey And I went outside.

Ian Straight outside?

Stueey Where was I when you came out?

Ian Outside.

Stueey There you are then!

Ian What're we gonna do now then?

Stueey Keep quiet. No one knows we were there.

Ian Molly?

Stueey Apart from Molly.

Ian And Shuttle. You said Shuttle saw you.

Stueey Well he didn't!

13 Burnt Fingers

IAN You said he did.

STUEEY He didn't!

IAN How do you know?

STUEEY He just didn't! Anyway he was too busy on his like go-kart thing!

IAN What?

STUEEY When I was outside waiting for you he was like riding around ... real cool.

IAN What about the CCTV?

STUEEY What do you mean?

IAN It'll've picked us up!

STUEEY Nothing ever shows up on that! Anyway we had our hoods up most of the time.

IAN It's a school, they're gonna really ...

STUEEY It didn't look like there was that much damage!

IAN Did to me!

STUEEY It's only a fire!

IAN Only?

STUEEY Wasn't even very big!

IAN It was big enough. A few minutes later and we could have been caught in it.

STUEEY Well, we weren't.

IAN I know this sounds stupid ... but ...

STUEEY If it sounds stupid don't bother saying it!

IAN I reckon we should go to the Old Bill and say we were there.

STUEEY You are a complete prat! I can't believe you're saying that Ian!

IAN But if we've got nothing to hide?

13 Burnt Fingers

STUEEY So we say we broke in and were throwing paper darts round ... and lighting them?

IAN I don't mean that but ...

STUEEY It'll put us right in the frame ...

IAN At least we won't be ...

STUEEY We can't!

IAN We should!

STUEEY Just shut it before I ...

IAN (*Scared, he reassures* **Stueey**.) I won't say anything ... not unless you do ... but ...

STUEEY Dork!!

IAN Me?

STUEEY Yeh.

IAN What about you wanting to stay there to watch?

STUEEY I told you, it'd've looked much stranger if we'd run away. I mean everyone was standing there looking. I wanted to get on TV and do a sob story about all my valuable course work going up in flames ... that would have been a real laugh .... (*In a mock posh voice*.) 'All that effort I put in going up in smoke!' (*He laughs*.) Wicked eh?

Pause.

IAN Stueey? Those notes ... was it you?

STUEEY What?

IAN You heard!

STUEEY Might've been.

IAN It was wasn't it?

STUEEY But I didn't set the fire!

IAN Why did you write them?

13 Burnt Fingers

Stueey   What do you think?

Ian   To scare Butcher?

Stueey   It was his fault I got excluded.

Ian   And before that? 'Cos there were some before you were kicked out weren't there.

Stueey   I don't know ... I'm not a bloody psychologist!

Ian   Butcher, Butcher Burning bright ... Stu ... why?

Stueey   It's like based on an old rhyme ...

Ian   Stueey? I didn't torch the school ... So who did?

Stueey   (*Angry.*) It could have been anything ... an electrical fault! Anything could have happened!

Ian   But it didn't, did it?

*****Stueey** approaches **Ian** and swings at him. **Ian** catches his punch.*

You don't scare me any more. Hit me if you want, but it won't do any good! I know you did it ... but I won't say anything 'cos I can't prove it!

Stueey   You say anything and you're dead!

Molly   And so it continues, arguments and more arguments. The whole thing is like surreal and then a few moments later, sirens and ... running and ... panic and ... oh no ... those words ... those words I'd heard on telly ... never thought I'd hear them like this!

Police 1 and 2   You are both under arrest on suspicion of murder.

Molly   Murder?

Police 1   You are not obliged to say anything, but it may harm your defence if you do not mention when questioned something which you later rely on in court. Anything you do say may be given in evidence.

IAN (*As himself.*) Someone's been killed? Killed in the fire? Who … who is it? It's not a girl is it? It's not Molly Dukes? Please … just tell me it's not Molly Dukes!

STUEEY You can't do nothing. You ain't got no evidence!

Ian and *Stueey* freeze.

MOLLY Both are carted off like … like criminals, and I feel, given the situation … strangely defensive. I'm certain neither of them had meant to do anything but if they have actually done something … well they can't be murderers … they can't be my murderers! But there was no time to dwell on that because suddenly with powers Shuttle's old Nan would have been really proud of, I beam myself up in his little cottage, which proves, against all expectations to be a beautiful little place and very clean … very, very clean.

I sit on the stairs and watch as Shuttle arrives home and his Nan greets him at the door. She's different to how I'd imagined … but then, I don't think she could ever have been as creepy as we'd all made out! I feel a bit bad actually.

Ian and *Stueey* exit.

14 SCARRED

NAN (*Greeting* **Shuttle**.) William dear … where … ? It's so late? There's been a fire at the school.

SHUTTLE I saw it.

NAN Big one?

SHUTTLE Not massive.

NAN But there was an explosion wasn't there?

SHUTTLE Not really!

NAN They said there was.

SHUTTLE Who?

14 Scarred

NAN The news.
SHUTTLE It's been on the news?
NAN The local news, yes.
SHUTTLE It wasn't really an explosion.
NAN I can smell petrol.
SHUTTLE Spilt it on my coat.
NAN What've you been doing with petrol.
SHUTTLE Our go-kart. Finished it tonight. We're keeping it at the school ... but nowhere near the fire.
NAN Won't they mind?
SHUTTLE Don't know. You should see it Nan. It's real fast.
NAN I'm worried love.
SHUTTLE What about?
NAN Your coat?
SHUTTLE What about it?
NAN The petrol.
SHUTTLE It'll wash out.
NAN That's not the point.
SHUTTLE Nan, can you wash it?
NAN In the morning dear.
SHUTTLE I need it done before.
NAN (*Pausing.*) You saw the fire?
SHUTTLE Slime had to call the fire brigade.
NAN Don't call him that. Is he alright?
SHUTTLE He says he saw some kids.
NAN What?
SHUTTLE Ones who set the fire.

14 Scarred

NAN Set the ... ?

SHUTTLE Started it Nan.

NAN Andrew was there?

SHUTTLE He was on duty.

NAN Won't he be coming home?

SHUTTLE He's still down the police station.

NAN What?

SHUTTLE Evidence.

NAN I hope he's not ... I hope you're not in trouble.

SHUTTLE The police'll 'phone.

NAN They been already.

SHUTTLE He said they would.

NAN Who?

SHUTTLE Slime.

NAN Andrew!

SHUTTLE They're not blaming me are they?

NAN Why would they?

SHUTTLE I was there ... kind of ...

NAN What do you mean.

SHUTTLE People ... they make stuff up. What did you say?

NAN What do you mean?

SHUTTLE To the police.

NAN I said you weren't at home. Is that the right thing to say?

SHUTTLE It's the truth.

14 Scarred

NAN The policeman ... he was a detective ... plain clothes ... he said I should 'phone him when you got back. Gave me his mobile number he did!

SHUTTLE You going to?

NAN Do you want me to?

SHUTTLE Up to you.

NAN What should I do with your coat dear?

SHUTTLE (*Handing it to her.*) I want you to wash it ... the petrol.

NAN I don't think I should.

SHUTTLE Why?

NAN Might look suspicious ... if they come round. (*Silence.*) Whatever has happened William ... I'll be with you ... I'll always stick by you.

SHUTTLE What are you on about Nan? I'm tired. I'm gonna go to bed.

Shuttle exits. **Nan** *picks up the 'phone and dials.*

NAN Could I speak to, erm, DC Brian O'Neill ... yes ... Hello, is that DC O'Neill? ... Yes, he has ... not much, no ... right ... just says he didn't see a thing. Thank you. (*She replaces the receiver very slowly.*)

MOLLY Poor old lady. She hangs Shuttle's coat up and then she goes over to the cupboard and (*disbelieving*) ... gets some polish out and starts polishing the table ... hard. Every now and then she stops to wipe her eyes. I want to tell her that I don't think Shuttle has anything to do with it ... but I can't be sure ... and anyway she won't hear me. When the doorbell finally rings she wipes her eyes, puts the polish away, looks up the stairs and opens the front door.

The very next moment I feel myself zooming away again ... time and space ... my watch whizzing round

14 Scarred

a full twelve rotations ... I'm taken to a room ... a white room ... and there in the middle of it is a body laid out under a sheet. The door's opening. Oh my God! Why oh why have I come to see this?

Dad!

The mortuary.

*A **Mortuary Attendant** lifts a sheet off the body. **Chris**, who is accompanied by DS Ford, looks down at the body. He moves away.*

CHRIS Yes that's our Molly. (*Showing signs of becoming upset.*) I'm sorry.

MOLLY Dad!

CHRIS (*To the **Mortuary Attendant**.*) I'll never understand how this happened.

*ced**Molly** stands still in the middle of the stage appealing to him.*

MOLLY Dad wait ... it wasn't your fault ...

CHRIS I had a dream last night ... a nightmare. Molly was alive and she came up to me and said, 'Why did you have to make me fit in with your life?'

MOLLY I wouldn't have said that. Dad, that wasn't me!

CHRIS I guess she thought I took her for granted.

MOLLY You're talking like I did it on purpose.

CHRIS My final moments with her were spent rowing. Rowing! We never row normally. Never rowed. Just laughed. Lots of laughs together. It shouldn't have been like that. Words eh?

MOLLY It was my fault too ... I should have ...

CHRIS Like that fire really ...

MOLLY What?

CHRIS Words ... words can be so powerful. (*To **Molly**.*) They will find whoever did it? They will won't they?

14 Scarred

Molly Dad! But he fades. Please, I don't want that to be the last I see of him. Be happy Dad ... send Mum my love. Tell her I'm sorry. Tell her not to worry. Tell her I'll be fine! But the scenery continues to change. A different room ... a table ... (*A table is brought on stage.*) ... two chairs ... (*Two chairs brought on stage.*) ... DC Ford ... the one who spoke to Mum and Dad last night ... (*looks at watch*) ... the clocks are going mental ... a whole day has passed ... and now Ian ... with two other people ... official looking ... and his Dad ... his poor Dad. They look so scared.

Molly is now looking at an interview room in a police station.

DC Ford (*Shows **Ian** the letter written to Butcher.*) Do you know what this is?

Ian No.

Silence.

Ian's Dad Ian, do you know anything about it?

Ian I said no, didn't I?

DC Ford (*Reading.*) 'Butcher, Butcher burning bright ... look around you'll see your kids alight.'

Silence.

Do you know Mr Butcher?

Ian He's my teacher.

DC Ford (*Pause.*) Did you write this letter?

Ian No.

DC Ford (*Pause.*) Have you ever touched this letter?

Ian What?

DC Ford (*Pause.*) Have you ever touched this letter?

Silence.

Ian's Dad Ian?

14 Scarred

DC Ford It was found in a part of the school building that wasn't affected by the fire. I have to inform you that the fingerprints on the letter have been matched to yours Ian.

Pause.

I'd like you to try and explain to me how your fingerprints came to be on this letter.

Ian I didn't write it though … honestly.

DC Ford But you did touch it?

Ian (*Pause.*) Yes. I didn't write it though.

DC Ford The letter was found in the school …

Ian I didn't write it!

DC Ford Who did then?

Ian (*Pause.*) I can't say.

Ian's Dad Just tell them what you know …

Ian I can't.

DC Ford Why? Are you scared of someone?

Silence.

It's Stueey isn't it?

Silence.

We've spoken to Stueey. He told us that you wrote the letter.

Ian What?

DC Ford He said you wrote the threatening letter to Mr Butcher. We've got it all on tape. I can play it to you if you like. Stueey has told us that you wrote those letters. Did you?

Ian No. I didn't.

DC Ford So you're saying Stueey's lying.

Silence.

14 Scarred

DC Ford Stueey also told us that you made one of these. (*He brings out a paper aeroplane.*)

Ian What?

DC Ford Stueey told us you made one of these.

Ian He suggested it!

DC Ford When?

Ian When? In the classroom. We'd got into this classroom … in B block … Stueey got us in … he emptied paper out and then said to me to make a paper aeroplane.

DC Ford Was this the only paper aeroplane you made?

Ian What do you mean?

DC Ford You said you made this in the school?

Ian Yeh.

DC Ford That same evening?

Ian Yeh. Why?

DC Ford A paper aeroplane just like this was found at the scene of another fire earlier in the day.

Ian What?

Pause.

I don't know nothing about that … honest I don't. We were … we did … (*Pausing.*) I wish I'd died in that fire too … I really wish I had!

DC Ford Why do you say that?

Long silence.

Ian (*Breaking down.*) I want to be with my Mum again. She'd know what to do … what to say. Me? I never do. All I know is that … well I'm not even sure that … see … we were just messing around!

Stueey *enters hesitantly.*

Stueey Is it OK if I do a monologue? It won't be that long and it'll be my last one … honest.

14 Scarred

DC Ford   Now Ian, we're gonna leave you here in this cell while we interview Stueey again. He says he wants to talk.

Stueey   (*To **DC Ford**.*) I'm not ready to do it as a statement yet. I'm just trying to sort things out in my mind. Can I be on my own? Just for a minute?

DC Ford   Go ahead.

Stueey   Thanks. (*He adopts his position as **Ian** and **DC Ford** observe out of role.*)

Ian won't be pleased when he comes to hear what really happened ... 'cos he set that fire he did. I know, 'cos I went back when he was looking for Molly. I was only there for a moment but, see, he'd thrown a lighted dart into the room, just before we left. I reckon it probably caught on some paper.

I went back to see. It had taken so I stayed and watched for a bit ... just for a moment. It wasn't that big then but (*with increasing pleasure*) I could see it getting bigger ... getting brighter ... getting hotter. I'll be honest with you ... I didn't want it to be found. I wanted to let it get bigger ... brighter ... hotter. I didn't think anyone was still inside. I didn't even think about that. If I had done I could've maybe done something. But I didn't. I thought she'd gone ages before. I only stayed a moment ... then straight outside. I wanted to see it from outside. I got outside for the like little explosion. Well, first I 'phoned 999 and told them. They said they'd been told already but they thanked me for my help. I was only inside watching for a moment ... I had to get out to meet up with Ian. I had no idea Molly was in there. (*Pausing.*) I only stayed a moment. It was glowing. Amazing. (*He turns to look at **Ian** and **DC Ford**.*)

DC Ford   Finished?

Stueey   Yeh. Was it OK?

DC Ford   Do you want to make an official statement?

14 Scarred

STUEEY   I ain't got nothing to say to you lot!

IAN   Will you be interviewing me after 'cos, well, we were just messing about … that's all it was … being prats!

DC FORD   It's gone way beyond that son … someone's dead … we could be looking at murder here.

Sound of a cell door shutting.

MOLLY   Like my dad said Ian, words are very powerful, like fire, very powerful.

*The **Chorus** enter to lead **Molly** off the stage.*

You've got to use that power Ian … you've got to say what you did … and what you saw Stueey do … and maybe what you think he did. You've got to speak out! Be bold … don't hide anything … and if … if what Stueey says is true you've got to face up to it Ian …

Hey … no … I haven't finished. Everything's fading … I'm fading! I wasn't expecting this to happen so suddenly … Can't I see Mum and Dad just once more?

I don't think I can hear any more … can you hear me Ian … can you? I hope you are innocent Ian … and no matter what you've got to speak! Ian … you've got to tell him everything you know … please Ian … please … just speak to him! (*She exits.*)

IAN   (*Shouting as though down the corridor to **DC Ford**.*) I never thought it would all turn out like this.

Silence.

We were just messing about that's all it was.

STUEEY   Yeh.

Pause.

Just arsing about.

THE END

ACTIVITIES

Things to talk about

1. You may have found *Arson About* to be very different from other plays you have read because of the number of different performance styles required. Some scenes should be fast and funny when performed; others need to be quieter to make them moving. Some scenes require an imaginative and very physical performance; some a more intense and sensitive treatment.

   Talk about which scenes or moments in the play seem to you to fit into the following genres of theatre:

   - *Naturalism*: the drama captures the mood and dialogue of life as it really is.

   - *Physical theatre*: the performers use their bodies to represent ideas, emotions and actions.

   - *Thriller*: the audience are given just enough hints about who may be responsible for a crime to keep them watching and guessing.

   - *Pastiche*: this is where the drama deliberately mocks something by copying some of its typical elements.

   - *Pantomime*: some typical elements of pantomime include direct address (that is, actors talking directly to the audience) and showing or saying things on stage that would logically be impossible in real life.

2. By drawing on a wide range of performance styles and theatrical genres such as these, the play conveys a number of different moods.

   - Skim through the play again and find words to describe the different moods as they occur. For example, you might decide that Scene 1 Embers is 'mysterious'. Scene 2 Combustible Material starts 'soppy' then becomes a little 'sad' when Ian talks about his mum.

- How would you describe the mood at the end of the play? How do you think an audience would feel having watched it all?

- Does the comedy of the earlier scenes help to create a sense of tragedy at the end, or do you think it is misleading and will confuse an audience when they don't get a happy ending?

3 An important part of building any dramatic character is to identify what motivates them, that is, giving them a reason for doing what they do in the drama. Sometimes characters just have one straightforward reason for doing something but at other times there may be a mixture of things that have caused them to act in the way they do. What are your ideas about:

- Why Molly goes with Ian and Stueey to the school

- Why Ian seems so impressed by Stueey

- Why Stueey 'arses' around so much

- Why Shuttle is such an outsider.

4 How do you feel about Ian and Stueey at the end of the play? Are they both equally responsible for what has happened or should one of them take more blame than the other?

5 In Scene 13 Burnt Fingers, Stueey mocks young people who would feel bad about their school burning down because, for example, all of their work would be destroyed. What effect would it have on you if your school was burnt down? What effect, do you think, would it have on the community?

6 Arson attacks on schools cost more than £1 million each week in Britain. Every day three schools are damaged or destroyed by arson. What do you think could be done to tackle such a massive problem?

Things to write about

7. The stage direction at the start of Scene 2 Combustible Material suggests that the scene should remind the audience of a photo-love story from a teen magazine. In a production of the play, it would be entertaining to project images of Ian and Molly getting together in the style of a photo-love story.

- Fold a piece of A4 paper in half three times. This will give you eight rectangular frames. Draw a line across the bottom of each row.

	Aaah Aaah	Molly Dukes! Yes, Sir?	
Stapping School. Mr Butcher's weekly detention	Our heroes …		

- Use this framework to draw a simple storyboard of Scene 2. Use the lower panel to write in the Narrator's lines (or make up your own) then draw simple stick figures, thought bubbles and speech balloons to tell the story.
- It would be fun to use a digital camera to record the images on your storyboard and use a personal computer to add the thought bubbles and speech balloons. The next step would be to put your story onto PowerPoint®.

8 The fire at the school would no doubt be reported on the local news. Quite often, local news items are structured in the following way:

- The story is introduced by the newsroom anchor person who will be reading a prepared speech from the autocue device.
- The anchor person will then hand over to an 'on-the-spot' reporter who will describe the scene and events. They would have prepared what they are going to say but probably wouldn't have actually written it down and learnt it.
- The reporter will often interview an eye-witness. Their talk is spontaneous as they simply try to answer the reporter's questions.
- Imagine that a local news report was included in the script of *Arson About*. Write the scene using the guidelines above for each of the different characters involved. Try to capture the difference between a speech that is being read, talk that has been prepared and spontaneous talk.
- Video record your presentations. Watch the recording and discuss how well each group captured the style of a local news report.

9   There are a number of things that people do when they speak spontaneously that they wouldn't generally do when they write something. Playwrights recognise this and try to capture the sense of 'real' speech when they are writing dialogue. One of the devices we use when we are talking is called ellipsis. This means that we don't speak in full sentences because there are things about the situation we are in that speak for themselves. For example, at the start of the play the cashier simply says, 'Pump 12?' instead of, 'Are you paying for the petrol you have just had from pump 12?'

- Find at least two more examples in the play where ellipsis is used to make the dialogue feel authentic.

- Write a short piece of dialogue on your own in which two characters are having a conversation about something they are doing but are not say exactly what they are doing because, to them, it will be obvious what they are talking about. Put a stage direction at the start of your piece to help the reader understand the context. For example:

Two surgeons in an operating theatre looking at a patient on the operating table.

SURGEON 1   Hmmmm! Cut?

SURGEON 2   Have to.

SURGEON 1   Going in ... deep and long.

SURGEON 2   Need to clamp open.

SURGEON 1   Lot's of blood.

SURGEON 2   Ah! Forgotten something.

SURGEON 1   Blast! Anaesthetic! (*To patient.*) Sorry!

10 In Scene 2 Combustible Material, Molly sends a text message to Ian. The language of text messaging, by telephone or MSN, is an entirely new form of writing. It

takes ellipsis one stage further by cutting out letters in the trust that the reader will understand the shortened version of a word. Not only that, text messaging sometimes uses pictorial devices such as smiley or frowning faces to convey meaning.

Write out a text message conversation for one of the following scenarios:

- Molly and Ian are both sitting at the back of Mr Butcher's class but on opposite sides of the room. Bored by the lesson they decide to text each other …

- Stueey texts Ian to taunt him about his relationship with Molly. Ian replies …

- Shuttle and Slime prepare to try out their go-kart by text …

- After Molly's funeral Ian receives a text message from … Molly! What sort of conversation would follow from that?!

11 Perhaps the most enigmatic character in the play, that is, the one we understand the least, is Shuttle.

- Look back at Scenes 1, 4 and 14. Draw a simple outline to represent Shuttle. Inside the figure, jot down what you know about him from these scenes.

- Now look at Scene 8. In the space outside the figure, jot down what other people think about him or think they know about him.

- If Shuttle could speak directly to the audience as Stueey does, what would he tell them about himself and the way he is regarded by the other characters? Write a monologue for him.

12 The script of *Arson About* is broken up into units or scenes. Each one has been given a caption type heading which suggests the mood and purpose of the scene. You will have noticed that each of these headings is related to an image

of burning. In fact, the play contains a great many images of fire and burning which serve a variety of functions.

- Find at least three other examples in the play where images of fire are used. Jot down what these images are and briefly explain what sort of job each one does in the context of the scene.
- Use a thesaurus to look up other words that mean the same as, or relate to, fire and burning.
- Invent a piece of dialogue that incorporates as many of these words as possible. Alternatively, use the words as the basis of a shape poem about fire.

13 *Arson About* makes good use of *juxtaposition* to create interesting theatrical moments. One example of juxtaposition is where different types of speech are inter-cut. For example, in Scene 3 Laying the Fuse, Molly and her parents are chatting around the family table but their conversation is inter-cut with Molly's thoughts and also words that describe what is happening. Similarly, when DC Ford breaks the news of Molly's death in Scene 12 The Smoke Clears, naturalistic dialogue is replaced by odd words which capture what the characters are thinking and doing rather than actually saying.

- Look at these two scenes again and discuss how this technique adds to the dramatic effect and makes the scene more theatrically interesting.
- Working on your own or in groups, write three contrasting speeches:
    - **a** Chris's talk to the congregation at Molly's funeral;
    - **b** An extract from Molly's diary in which she talks about her hopes for the future;
    - **c** A letter from Ian explaining his part in Molly's death and how he feels about it.
- Find a way of inter-cutting the three speeches so that the different feelings they contain are dramatically juxtaposed.

Bringing the play to life

14 Many of Mark Wheeller's plays provide performers with great opportunities to work physically to bring scenes to life by using their bodies to represent things rather than using sets and stage furniture. When he is working with actors himself, Mark uses the term 'body-props' to describe this technique of personifying objects, that is, representing things as if they were somehow human.

- Talk about any films or cartoons you know that use this technique, for example, Walt Disney's *Beauty and the Beast*.

- One way of deciding how to create a body-prop is to think of the physical properties of the object that you wish to represent. For example, think of a grandfather clock. Is it light or heavy? Young or old? Bright or dull? Having made your decisions, try and stand in a way that shows these physical properties. Imagine that, by the magic of theatre, the grandfather clock could move and speak. How would it move? How would it speak and what would it say?

- Working in groups, devise a short scene in which a number of inanimate objects come to life (think of *Toy Story*!). Remember, the main purpose is to show physically what their characteristics are and to use your voices accordingly.

15 Some of the scenes in *Arson About* demand that members of the cast work together physically to create things, for example, in the fairground scene the performers will need to find a way of showing a rifle range, a roller-coaster and a test-of-strength machine.

Work in small groups of five or six to see if you can make:

- a cuckoo clock
- a food mixer
- a car with doors that open, seat belts, windscreen wipers, radio, electric aerial …

16 A technique similar to the body-props exercise is to make an 'essence machine' of a situation.

- Work in groups of five or six. Each one of you should think of a line that captures something about school. For example, 'Oh great! Physics next!' 'Helen, just sit still and stop doing that!' or 'I'm never gonna get this homework done.'

- Now put a simple action to your line that you can repeat over and over again.

- The next job is put the lines and actions together in a way that shows mechanically a number of different aspects of school. Your machine ought to be able to go faster or slower and get louder or quieter.

17 How could you use ideas such as body-props, personification and essence machines to show something horrific like a fire starting and getting out of control? As you devise and rehearse, keep thinking about the effect you want to have on your audience.

18 In contrast to the fast, furious and quite whacky theatre created by this kind of physicalisation, *Arson About* also presents the audience with some quite difficult, uncomfortable and emotive conversations. This is another example of juxtaposition. In this case, dramatic effect is achieved by suddenly switching the mood and atmosphere.

- Pick at least two moments in the play where you think the audience could be made to feel quite emotionally involved with the characters. Read them through carefully and talk about what makes these scenes emotive. Is it what the characters are talking about, or the way they are talking about them? Very possibly, it is a combination of both.

- In pairs, devise a short scene in which a character has to break a bad piece of news to another character. Once again, it is important to keep thinking about how you want the audience to feel.

- Difficult situations can be made even more dramatic by adding irony, for example when a character thinks that they are in one situation when really they are in another. In groups, try to bring the following scenario to life.

> Some adults are having a Christmas fancy dress party. Everyone is having a good time and they are all getting just a wee bit drunk. The doorbell rings and someone enters dressed as a police officer. Everyone at the party thinks it's a great outfit. The trouble is that it is a real police officer who has come to inform one of the adults that their son or daughter has just been killed in a drink-drive accident.

- Talk about what challenges you faced to bring this scene to life. How did you manage to change the mood from something quite comic to something very painful?

STAGING THE PLAY

20 Although the script of *Arson About* is broken down into units, the play should run straight through without any obvious breaks. However, some scenes will need a minimal amount of stage furniture and different lighting.

- Skim through the script again and make a chart like the one shown below to record how each scene might be set quickly and easily. You may decide that the lights need to change during the scene.

Scene	Location	Set/Props	Lighting
1	A petrol station	Small table for counter	
		Wheelbarrow	
		Petrol can	Orange glow for street lighting
2	Classroom	School chairs for Molly and Ian	Pink, romantic wash
3			
4			

21 At the end of Scene 1, the playwright suggests that music is used to change the atmosphere.

- How many songs can you think of that make some sort of reference to fire? *The Guinness Book of Hit Singles* will prove a good source of ideas for this.

- Where else in the play do you think it would be useful to use pre-recorded music to set the atmosphere?

22 Scene 7 Fireworks at the Fair presents particular challenges for the performers who must work together to capture all of the business and fun of the fair by being both people there and the fairground attractions themselves.

- Divide into five groups. One group should work on building the essence of the fairground by using the Stall-Holders' lines (add as many more of your own as you please). One group should find a way of representing the 'hook the duck' attraction and another the 'rifle range'. A third group should work out how to show the roller-coaster and fourth a waltzer. The fifth group will need to show the 'test-of-strength machine'.

- Try to put the whole sequence together from the start of the scene to Molly's line on page 36 'The magic of theatre!' Remember, the whole scene needs to move at breakneck speed but it must be absolutely clear to an audience what is going on.

23 In contrast to the fun and madness of the fairground scene, Scene 11 Arson About?, uses the Chorus to create a sense of fear and panic. Once again, the lines need to be played at a tremendous pace but the atmosphere should be altogether darker.

- In groups of four, read from where Molly first goes off on her own to the end of the scene (pages 54–59).

- Experiment with using your voices in different ways by, for example, changing the volume and tone.

- Choose one short section of between 12–20 lines. Try to learn the lines then devise a sequence of movements to help capture the growing tension. Once again, bear in mind the effect you want to have on an audience.

24 The relationship between Molly and Ian is central to the play and reflects how something that starts as a bit of fun can grow into something too serious and finally gets out of control.

- In pairs, rehearse the following three extracts:

    a From Ian's line 'I want to text her (page 11) – Molly's second 'Yeh!' (page 12)

    b From Molly's line 'Ian!' (page 25) to Molly's and Ian's line 'a very sticky end!' (page 27)

    c From Molly's line 'Why the hell have I got myself involved in this?' (page 49) to her line 'Ian … don't …please, …just stay down.' (page 50)

- Discuss how Molly's and Ian's relationship changes from each one of these scenes to the next. Choose just two lines from each scene which you think sums up the relationship at that point. How should the characters be positioned when they say these lines to emphasise the nature of their relationship at that moment?

25 The character of Shuttle is described as 'an individualistic teenager'. Not only is he an outsider at the school, he is also a sort of outsider in the main story of *Arson About*. That's not to say he doesn't have a very important function in the play.

- Discuss what impression an audience will get of Shuttle at the start of the play. What assumptions will they make about him?

- How does the audience's impression of him change by the end of the play and how does this change come about?

- In groups of three, read through Scene 1 Embers and Scene 14 Scarred. Decide how you want the audience to feel about Shuttle by the end of each of these scenes then, using one of your group as a director, rehearse the scenes to try and create this effect.

- Discuss what dramatic purpose do you think the character of Shuttle has.

EXPLORING THE ISSUES

26 Schools are the most arson prone buildings in the UK. Many of the attacks start in refuse bins, sheds and around doors and alcoves. The danger increases at the end of term when staff clear out rubbish and bins overflow with unwanted displays and piles of paper.

- Conduct a 'risk assessment' of your school to identify the places which you think might be most vulnerable to this sort of vandalism.

- Draw up an 'action plan' to suggest ways that security might be improved to lessen the risk of attack in these areas.

Act One

- A good site for finding out more about how arson endangers education and what can be done to tackle the problem is:
  http://www.arsonpreventionbureau.org.uk

Here is an extract from the site:

> The fire was discovered at 00.39hrs. The block, which was almost completely destroyed, housed 16 teaching rooms, the library, main office, pastoral offices, the head and deputy's offices and the staff room. The history and geography departments were completely wiped out whilst the modern languages, mathematics, English, special educational needs and RE departments lost many resources.
>
> The trauma and devastation was summed up by the head teacher:
>
> 'The first reaction is shock and numbness, followed by total disbelief and then realisation that 25 years of resources had gone; that all the carefully collected photographs, booklets and artefacts from all over Europe had gone; that all paperwork for the administration of public examinations had gone, and all the school text books and personal belongings had gone.'
>
> The timing of the fire was particularly unfortunate, since Year 9 SATs were to be held later in the week and GCSE examinations were due to begin within a month.

- In groups, use this statement as the basis for a piece of drama of your own devising. Try to capture the 'trauma and devastation' that resulted from the loss of 25 years worth of work and effort.